Rooted & Restored

Finding God in Undesirable Soil

By Melia Chapman

Copyright © 2025 Melia Chapman, All rights reserved.

ISBN-13:979-8-218-66562-3

Instagram: @melia.rae.chapman
Contact: jmhcchapman@gmail.com

All scripture references are from the ESV translation, unless otherwise noted.

English Standard Version Bible. (2001). ESV Online.
https://esv.literalword.com/
Peterson, E. (2018). *The Message: The Bible in Contemporary Language.* NavPress

Calligraphy and graphics contributed by Charity Wilhite, sketch artist.
Poems written and contributed by Christine DeMoss, poet.
Cover design by Lia Gilland, graphic designer.
Book design and line-editing by Bethany Duarte, editor
dba *Modern Day Wordsmith*.

Dedication

To you who hold this book right now – the searching soul, the hurting heart, the devastated dreamer. You are the reason I wrote this book. I know your pain. I do. But I also know that God sees you. He's a good Gardener and the caretaker of your soul. He promises that He can be found in soil just like this – in everything that feels undesirable. Nothing is wasted in His hands. Keep bringing Him all that you have, even when it feels like nothing remarkable. You'll faithfully receive His everything. My prayer is that you will become deeply rooted to Him in life-giving and restoring ways as you embrace the truths throughout these pages.

To Hunter, Case, and Hattie Pearl:
May you always see the value of tethering yourself to Jesus. And may you always see the beauty in every piece of your story.

Introduction   1

PART ONE: PLANTED

Chapter 1	Buried	5
Chapter 2	Good Plans	17
Chapter 3	Purpose in Your Placement	27
Chapter 4	Kool-Aid & Tomato Plants	35
Chapter 5	I'll Have What He's Having	43

PART TWO: GROWING

Chapter 6	Preparing the Soil	54
Chapter 7	Seeds That Get Snatched	69
Chapter 8	Seeds That Get Scorched	80
Chapter 9	Seeds That Get Choked	93
Chapter 10	Seeds That Get Sabotaged	103
Chapter 11	100-Fold	112

PART THREE: PRUNING

Chapter 12	Renaming the Soil	122
Chapter 13	Abiding	132
Chapter 14	The God Who Sees	145
Chapter 15	New Skin	164
Chapter 16	He is in the Fire	179
Chapter 17	Remnants From the Ruins	189

PART FOUR: FLOURISHING

Chapter 18	Proof is in the Fruit	201
Chapter 19	Take Me There	208
Chapter 20	His Touch	219
Chapter 21	Manasseh & Ephraim	232
Chapter 22	The Manna Lifestyle	239
Chapter 23	Cedars of Lebanon	245

A note from Melia   257
Acknowledgements   263
About the Author   266

The world offers so many counterfeits.
So many of us are wrongly rooted.

My heart's desire is to help people discover the beauty woven inside of them when their identity is rooted in Christ, and for them to see the move of His hand over every detail of their lives, even in the most painful of places.

Every cut holds a purpose.
Nothing is wasted.

— Melia

Introduction

Oftentimes, the greatest testament to our character is when we've walked through fire but don't smell like smoke.

We will walk through painful things, experience difficult seasons, and undergo trials that we never saw coming, never would have chosen, and quite honestly would love to escape. But that doesn't mean that the residue that remains has to smell like what we've been through.

There is a place for pouring your heart out to a trusted mentor and allowing that person to speak life into you.

That is biblical.

There is a place for carrying one another's burdens.

That is biblical.

There is a place for asking the prayer warriors in your life to touch the throne room of Heaven with you.

That is biblical.

And yet…

What if you walked through something indescribably painful and chose not to allow that pain to define you?

What if you experienced devastating betrayal, and instead of tainting the character of the offender, you chose to keep it private and let God do deeper work in you?

What if you found yourself up against insurmountable resistance, and instead of enrolling everyone you know to fight for you, you believe God for it?

What if instead of always feeling like your side of the story needs to be known, you invite God to be your greatest Defender?

What if, in the center of your deepest battle, when flaming arrows are flying toward you, you experience Him as your shield and deliverer?

What if instead of always needing things to be right, you found value in pursuing righteousness?

What if in the midst of the impossible, you trust God to come through and experience His provision in a way you never have before?

What if you found yourself in the deepest valley, and instead of inviting everyone you know to join you, it was just you and Him... and you found out He was enough?

It's hard to see the significance of the season you're in sometimes.
But there is power in silent sermons. There's a flourishing of fruit to be found in afflicting seasons.

When you don't smell like what you've been through, and when you've been through the fire, and you're not hardened because of it but refined instead, THAT is a testimony of what God can do with a soul who has surrendered to Him.

We have all been placed and positioned by God with a purpose for a purpose. We have all walked through seasons of deep growth as He has pruned, refined, and purified us.

My prayer is that through it all, you experience the joy of living a flourishing life under His care.

PART ONE
Planted

To place in the ground so that it can grow.
To fix in a specific position.

They will be called oaks of Righteousness—
a planting of the Lord for the display of His Splendor.
Isaiah 61:3

CHAPTER ONE
Buried

One of my first jobs after college and becoming a new mom was working as an office assistant at a welding company in the office department. It was a quiet place above the working welders down below. It gave me a lot of opportunities to listen to what God was speaking over my life in that season.

The majority of the workers at this company were men. If there is anything that I learned early on during my time there, it was that these men loved to play pranks on each other. It became a very entertaining place to work because of that. I got the opportunity to get an inside peek into all their shenanigans. I wasn't usually the one they picked on, but one particular day, as I was leaving work (late as usual to pick my kids up from school, mind you), I was greeted by the absence of my vehicle.

Panic instantly set in. Where is my van? I'm going to be late! This better not be a prank! After hunting down the guys I thought would be responsible for this, I found my vehicle tucked in and tightly surrounded by pallets. I quickly realized that I couldn't open any of the side doors. My only option was the back hatch, which I soon figured out was also locked. The only way to unlock that back hatch door was by opening the driver's door which was blocked in. I was buried–stuck. On my own, I couldn't get out. There was no way of escape!!

In an instant, there was this flashback. God brought me back. He brought me back to what seemed like a lifetime ago, and yet a memory that felt like yesterday all at once.

It is interesting how that works sometimes. A flash of a moment can, in one breath, feel like a lifetime ago, and yet it can feel so real and so raw that it almost takes your breath away.

God brought me back to probably the *most* transformative night in my spiritual journey to date. To the point in time when I was as lost and buried as my van was. It was the night He saved me from myself. It was the night that He saved me from the grips of hell. In one of the darkest moments of my life, in college dorm room 208 in a building called Stockton in Olathe, Kansas, I could feel the tight grip of despair over my life.

I was a freshman in college–barely 18. I got accepted to college on a soccer scholarship. Soccer was one of my few, deep loves at that time in life. God had given me the talent and ability to play the game with some natural talent. I recognized that. But only by the mercy of God did I even find myself at this beautiful Christian college surrounded by many people who loved Jesus.

I had grown up going to church. I knew a lot about Jesus. But knowing a lot about Jesus and knowing Jesus as your Savior are two distinctly different things. I knew and loved people who loved Jesus. I loved the idea of loving Jesus. Those are also two very distinctly different things. I guess you could say I was more of a fan than a follower. I knew a lot about God, but my life didn't reflect any part of Him. I wasn't pursuing Him like He was pursuing me. I had the foundation of a childhood spent learning about Him, but my eyes were on the world and the things of it. Every desire I had was being filled with the temporary pleasures of things the world could offer.

In short, I had a lot of brokenness.

I love the phrase and often quoted line: "God will pick up the pieces and put them back together." Christian author and speaker Lysa Terkeurst says: "Sometimes things in our life become so broken that there aren't parts to glue back together. The shattering is severe. There's just ashes. You can't glue ashes. The thing about dust and ashes, though, is that they are one of God's favorite ingredients. He could've chosen any ingredient for His favorite creation—us. And He chose to make us from dust. Dust doesn't signify the end. It is the necessary agent for the new to begin."

That night, as I looked around at the residue of my life, it felt final—down to just ashes. Things were falling apart all around me. There was brokenness everywhere I looked.

I was falling apart, too. Not due to one singular thought or circumstance but rather a culmination of every lie, every strategy of the enemy to come against my worth and my destiny. My mind felt blanketed by a thick cloud of oppression. My thoughts had become a prison filled with fear and anguish—unending pain, torment, and unrest. My thoughts were a mine field of anxiety, depression, hopelessness, insecurity and a deep-seeded lack of identity. There were seeds that had been sown into the field of my heart over many, many years. While they had no place growing there, I didn't have the tools then to know how to get rid of these oppressing thoughts or make them leave.

It was at this very moment when my spiritual life was standing on this outstretched cliff, and it felt like there was nowhere to turn. I was too scared to jump away from all I knew but too stubborn and tormented to stay in the chaos of it any longer.

I remember that night so vividly. Drenched in sweat from another hard practice, grass stains covering my white practice uniform, I was mentally exhausted at the thought of even facing all the chatter in my mind again and the continued ones that I knew would come. I was fearing more

When you're in a
dark place, you tend
to think you've been
buried.
What if you've been
planted instead?

than just my thoughts. I was fearing reality, too. Nothing really felt stable or secure in my life. It all felt like it could crumble with one breath blown.

Everything I feared was everything that I was living - familiarity and the unfamiliar married in the most painful way.

I remember falling on my face before God on that freezing night in October and crying out, "I hate You! I hate that You created me—for nothing. I hate myself. I don't even want to live anymore."

It was just me and God in that dorm room that night. This moment that first felt like the end became the birth of my beginning. He came to my rescue. I could feel Him literally pulling me out of this deep, black pit towards His glorious light.

This moment signifies the day He unburied me and pulled me out of my grave.

It wasn't a pretty process, though.

When gardeners grip their hands underneath hardened soil to pull something out, it leaves their hands dirty. The unburying isn't all that glamorous. Nothing about it is clean, but I know now that God isn't afraid of the mess.

He wasn't then. He isn't now. He isn't afraid to get His hands dirty.

He brought me back to Him that night.

When you're in a dark place, you sometimes tend to think you've been buried. Perhaps you are just beginning to be planted.

My salvation and deliverance story will always be my favorite story. It's the birth of everything else. Without it, nothing else really matters.

There's this young shepherd boy named David in the Bible who became the anointed King of Israel. David's life story is incredible. It even says that He was a man after God's own heart. Over time, David rose in strength and frame. He did honorable and remarkable things for the Lord. He built a small empire, conquered Jerusalem, defeated huge armies, slayed a giant, and moved the Ark of the Covenant. He was a builder, a commander, a ruler, and a king, but he was also human and sinful. He found himself repeatedly repenting before the Lord—crying out for deliverance. David found himself in a pit of destruction, too.

David's deliverance story is coined through these words:

> I waited patiently for the Lord. And He heard my
> cry. He brought me up out of that horrible pit and set
> my feet on solid ground. He established my steps and has
> put a new song in my mouth. I will trust the Lord.
> Psalm 40:1-3

God didn't leave David trapped down under in the dark. Sure, he had to stay there for a while, but God brought him out. David begged and pleaded with God to deliver Him, and He did.

He delivered me, and He promises to deliver you, too.

The persistence of a plea can deliver us from more than we probably even realize. I begged and pleaded persistently with the welders at work that afternoon to unbury my van, and the persistence of my pleas paid off. We all laughed about it for years to come afterward, but that particular day wasn't a laughing moment for me. It was a desperate one.

You may be in a place of desperation, too. You may be waiting on the Lord to pull you out of a pit of despair. I believe God turns His ear toward those who are passionately and desperately persistent in their pleas. God loves us so much that He rescues us from the grip of anything else that promises to satisfy but won't.

Read that again. *God loves us so much that He will rescue us from the grip of anything else that promises to satisfy us but doesn't.*

In Matthew 18:10-14, Jesus shares a parable about a shepherd leaving 99 sheep on a hill to search for the lost one. The Hebrew word for "lost" is "*abad*," which does not mean just to wander off but to ultimately perish.

His Word says in verse 14 that the God of Heaven is not willing for any to perish. He isn't willing. This single word, "abad," transforms the action of the Shepherd, Jesus. The Shepherd isn't merely finding something that has been misplaced. He is rescuing someone from dying. Without Jesus, our eternity is found in hell. This kind of love is hard for us to comprehend fully. It seems irrational to leave 99 behind to seek and save the lost.

It feels reckless…until you are the one.

This isn't just finding the lost one to recover it. It is rescuing to revive.

I remember being at my brother's house one summer when my boys were really young. My nephews, my sister, and her son were there that day, along with my boys and me. We often would get together in the summer and let the cousins play. This particular day was no different. The kids had ridden dirt bikes and four-wheelers earlier in the day. We decided to go inside and cool off from the hot summer sun.

My sister and I got busy visiting, and after some time had passed, we noticed that my 3-year-old son, Case, had gone missing.

"Kade, have you seen Case? Jax, Vinny. Have you guys seen Case?"

No one had seen him. Immediately we started searching the premises. Ten minutes had passed, and still no Case. My chest got heavy. My heart physically hurt knowing that my child was lost. I wasn't focusing on the other kids. My only gaze was on the one that was lost.

One of Case's favorite places was the stream way back in the woods at my brother's house.

My sister turned to me and said, "Melia, we have to pray."

Case didn't know how to swim all that well and really didn't know how to navigate the woods behind the house. He really could be anywhere. At that moment, I couldn't make myself even utter words. I frantically rushed off to hear my sister and nephews praying for Case to be found.

Literally seconds later, my oldest son, Hunter, came running from the woods with Case. He had one shoe on and one shoe off. We never did find where the other shoe ended up.

The anguish of a child lost, and the celebration of his being found are the lowest and highest of emotions of a parent. As I drove home that summer night, I looked in the rearview mirror to see that Case was snoring away. To remember that only moments prior, he was wandering and lost.

But he was found. Because he was searched for.

It's the heart of the seeking Shepherd that finds the one that is lost. There is more rejoicing in heaven over the one that was lost and has been found than over the 99 who do not need rescue.

Are you lost today?

I know what it feels like to be beyond reach. Our mistakes seem too many. Our wandering is too persistent. Our brokenness can feel too final. *When we wonder if we have finally been buried too deep, wandered beyond His reach, the move of God speaks.* The rescue is dependent entirely on the heart of the Shepherd. Nothing about the rescue has anything to do with the worthiness of the sheep. If that were so, there would be no sheep worthy of rescue. The heart of the Shepherd is actively seeking us with this crazy, death-defying love today.

Like a freshly planted seed, you may only see darkness right now. But it's the place you're going to find Him. It's the place you'll sprout your first leaf. It's the place you'll begin to grow. It's the soil He will use to bring forth so much goodness and fruitfulness in your life.

I pray you thank Him even when all you see is the darkness.

I pray that you thank Him even when the pain is deep.

More is happening underneath this dark season's soil than you can see. He hasn't forgotten about you.

If you've had an encounter where you experienced the Savior of the world pull you from the pits of despair and deliver you, I pray that that moment still feels like yesterday to you, too. I pray that that moment will be forever etched in your heart and mind as a promise of what He can redeem through the broken pieces.

If you are reading this and do not know Jesus Christ as your personal Lord and Savior, if you have not experienced His reckless Shepherd pursuit to find you in your wandering, I pray that you will take a moment to meditate on Matthew 18:12-14! He is pursuing you and offering you the greatest gift that you could ever be given through Him.

> If a man owns a hundred sheep, and one of them wanders away, will he not leave the ninety-nine on the hills and go to look for the one that is lost? And if he finds it, truly I tell you, he is happier about that one sheep than about the ninety-nine that were not lost. In the same way, your Father in heaven is not willing that any of these should perish.
> –Jesus in Matthew 18:12-14

Our sins separate us from God. Apart from God, we stay lost and broken and continue to sin. Without Him, we cannot experience true joy and the abundant life that He can offer us. Jesus Christ bridges the gap through His sacrificial death on the cross to cover our sins. Jesus Himself was buried for three days, according to the scriptures. He conquered death, hell, and the grave. Through Him, we can, too.

If you have never accepted Jesus Christ to be your personal Lord and Savior and would like to, take a few moments to read these verses.

- ❖ For all have sinned and come short of the glory of God. Romans 3:23. We have all sinned. We have all done things that are displeasing to God. None of us are without sin, so we all are in need of Jesus as our Savior.

- ❖ For the wages of sin is death. Romans 6:23a. The punishment we've earned for our sins is death. Not just physical death, but eternal death. An earthly life separated from Jesus leads us to an eternal death in hell apart from Him and our Father God.

- ❖ But the gift of God is eternal life through Jesus Christ our Lord…But God demonstrates His own love toward us, in that while we were still sinners, Christ died for us. Romans 6:23 b; 5:8. Jesus Christ died for us while we were still sinning! Jesus' death paid for the price of our sins, and His resurrection proves that God accepted His death as the payment for our sins. The resurrecting power of Jesus, through His obedience to take our sins to the cross once and for all, allows us to live a life of freedom, abundance, peace, and joy through Him.

- ❖ If you confess with your mouth Jesus as Lord and believe in your heart that God raised Him from the dead, you will be saved…Everyone who calls on the name of the Lord will be saved. Romans 10:9; 10:13. Because of Jesus' death on our behalf, all we have to do is believe in Him, trusting His death as the payment for our sins, and we will be saved! He came to UNBURY US! Salvation, the forgiveness of sins, is available to anyone who will trust in Jesus Christ as Lord and Savior.

- ❖ Therefore, since we have been justified through faith, we have peace with God through our Lord Jesus Christ. Romans 5:1. Through Jesus Christ, we can have a relationship of peace with God.

- ❖ Therefore, there is now no condemnation for those who are in Christ Jesus. Romans 8:1. Because of Jesus' death on our behalf, we can live in a right relationship with Jesus and be offered the gift of His Holy Spirit to be our counselor and friend on this earthly walk.

If you just read these words and believe in your heart, through faith, that Jesus Christ paid the price and penalty for your sins, you are saved. You have just accepted the gift of eternal life in Jesus Christ. Through faith in Jesus Christ, God's power can change you.

You don't have to live a life of brokenness and bondage.

You don't have to live without hope.

You are no longer lost.

You are found.

The Heavens are rejoicing. Jesus promises to walk alongside you on this journey and give you joy, peace, and hope.

REFLECT

- If you just accepted Jesus Christ as your personal savior, do you know someone who would be a good mentor and spiritual partner for you in this early stage of walking with Jesus? Take a moment today and reach out to that person, share the great news of your salvation, and ask him/her to come alongside you. If you cannot think of anyone, ask God to bring someone into your life who is equipped to take you deeper in this Jesus journey. You can also contact me personally. We all need to pair up with people who will sharpen and disciple us into a deeper relationship with Him.
- How does it feel to know that nothing can separate you from the love of Jesus? NOTHING! There is nothing you've done, nothing that has been done to you. There is no circumstance, nothing, that will separate you.
- In this season where you feel buried, how can you walk in newness of life? How can you praise Him and thank Him for where He has you—even if it feels foreign or unfamiliar? Thank Him even if it feels like you are buried in the dark.
- As God begins to unbury you, you will feel free and exposed–like the tiniest sprout of a seedling. Does that make you excited or nervous?

Journal some thoughts as you embrace where He has planted you in this season.

SCRIPTURE

A precious promise for you, my friend in the Lord:

> For I am convinced that neither death nor life, neither angels nor demons, neither the present nor the future, nor any powers, neither height nor depth, nor anything else in all creation, will be able to separate us from the love of God that is in Christ Jesus our Lord.
> Romans 8:38-39

PRAYER

Thank you, Lord, for offering us the gift of salvation through Your Son, Jesus. We cling to Your sovereignty today. Even if what we see in front of us doesn't feel good or look good, your plans are good. We may not understand the process, but we can trust You even in the uncertainty. Even if harm comes our way, you'll use it for good. When all we see is darkness, thank you for the hope we can find in you. We trust that you have our future planned out from the very beginning. Allow us to rest in you and rest in your master plan. Give us the confidence to find joy in the journey with you. In Jesus' name, Amen

CHAPTER TWO

Good Plans

> "For I know the plans I have for you," declares the Lord, "plans to prosper you and not harm you, plans to give you a hope and a future."
> Jeremiah 29:11

I'm going to destroy what this verse means to you, but then I'm going to reframe it so we can understand it within its original context. You will love it even more when we're done!

Here's the scene.

The Israelites were uprooted from Jerusalem. They'd been torn from their homes and taken to a foreign land in Babylon.

Ever feel like where God has placed you is so foreign? The soil is so unfamiliar. So much so that when you look around, you feel so out of place, like you don't belong? You wonder what God was thinking when He planted you here?

You're not alone. Where you are right now is not an accident.

God spoke to the survivors through the prophet Jeremiah, who sent a handwritten letter to the people.

> Build houses and live in them; plant gardens and eat their produce.
> Jeremiah 29:4-5

No one is instructed to build a house if they aren't supposed to stay a while. The concept of planting a garden in order to eat its produce encompasses multiple seasons. Both of these things take time, so we're not talking about a short stay.

God was telling them to make a home in a place they never wanted to be. He was telling them to bloom in a foreign, undesirable plot of land. It didn't just feel like captivity; it *was* captivity.

I can relate to this. We all can. There are just some seasons where your roots feel like they are in cement, and it's as hard and unmoving as granite. We desire rich, black soil, and where we are planted sometimes just doesn't feel that way under our feet.

The soil can be less than desirable.

NOW comes the famous passage from Jeremiah 29:11.

> "For I know the plans I have for you," declares the Lord, "plans to prosper you and not harm you, plans to give you a hope and a future."
> Jeremiah 29:11

Jeremiah 29:11 is God's promise and the foreshadowing of His plans to cause them to flourish right where they are. It's hard to believe that promise when you're in a place full of pain that doesn't look very prosperous. That promise looks like dry, barren clay. It's hard to believe that promise when He is asking you to stay in a place that feels devastating. It's hard to believe that promise when all you see around you is hurt, heartache, and hopelessness.

We can become choked out by what we can't see and what we don't know. We can become choked out by our thoughts, which tend to have a way of germinating like fast-growing weeds.

I know that. I've felt that. I've lived and experienced this very thing.

Another thing I do know: our placement isn't a mistake, and we aren't always called to escape. The Babylonian captivity was for the purpose of God dealing with sin in their lives. We can be saved and still be in bondage to sin in many areas of our lives. The Israelites were, too.

Think about these people who were forced to embrace wilderness seasons. They were asking, "Are we going right to the promised land?"

The promised land. The land flowing with milk and honey. The land of ease.

God's response, "No we are not. Right now, we are going through the wilderness."

Their captivity and exile were God's approach for them to become repentant and turn from their wickedness. Some were. Some received their placement, trusted that God had a purpose for it, and yielded to His desire for them to repent and turn away from every idol thing in their lives.

A large number of them still did not repent. They stayed in their place of exile, sure. But they became bitter. They cursed the soil they were in. The more that you read about the Israelites, the more that you see a narrative of them memorializing the past, even if it was bondage. They had an inability to even recognize when they were in bondage. They didn't surrender to His purpose for the "cold/winter season." It just became wasted time. This wasn't God's desire and heart for them in this season. They couldn't see past their own discomfort, controlling spirits and sin long enough to be refined.

We are the ones that get to choose whether we receive His purpose for the hard and harsh seasons, or whether we just "endure" them and become bitter through them.

We think it's annoying that God won't take us straight to the promised land where the soil is richer. We may not be called to long for something better. Rather, He may be calling us to invest and grow right where we are. He may be calling us to seek the welfare of a place where we never thought we'd be.

In my case, He was asking me to tend the soil of a field that felt unfair.

The soil He is asking you to tend may feel undesirable, painful, uncomfortable. So many adjectives describe the soil where He chooses to plant us sometimes.

Do we realize what we can experience if we would surrender to the soil He has us planted in?

We could experience His supernatural provision.

We could encounter His tangible leading and guiding as our Shepherd.

We could acquire an overabundance of peace.

But it won't happen for those who curse the soil and white knuckle what He's trying to do.

During this uprooted season in Babylon, God gave the Israelites this command:

> Seek the welfare of the city where I have sent you
> into exile and pray to the Lord on its behalf, for in its
> welfare, you will find your welfare.
> Jeremiah 29:7

Seeking the welfare of a place is so much more than just enduring a place. It is so much more than just putting up with people. Seeking the welfare of a place is a commitment to love and serve parts and people that are painful. We are called to maintain a faithful presence in an unfair world–in our jobs, our communities, and in our churches. We are called to carry out lives of obedience before God in front of a watching world.

It's not easy, friends. The easy route looks nothing like this. The easy route is shorter, less treacherous, and many days may feel more enticing. However, the destination is drastically different.

Before we go any further, I need to preface this: There are going to be days (or even seasons) when you question where God has planted, positioned, and placed you. You'll wonder if He has forgotten about you. You'll question whether He even sees your heartache. You'll desperately wish for something different.

There are going to be days when the weight seems so heavy, you really believe you may break. There are going to be days that no amount of problem-solving or strategy will take the struggle away. There aren't enough words or ways to answer the "why" behind every question your heart carries.

There are going to be days when the burnout level is so high, and you can't even find words to leave your lips.

There are going to be days when you feel forgotten, neglected, and overlooked. The invisibility factor will seem so real and so raw–like sandpaper on an open wound.

There are going to be days when you feel like everyone around you needs you but question whether anyone really wants you. The demands on you feel endless.

There are going to be days where you are tempted to dream of something different–not knowing that *that* life would come with its burdens, too.

There are going to be hard days, days that just feel like drought.

But what I pray you can see through it all is a Creator and Gardener who took careful, faithful discernment in the placement of your soul.

Some days and seasons are just not visibly flashy with budding blooms.

Friends, you don't have to be blooming to be growing.

Some seasons are for pruning, weeding, watering, and cultivating. Where we are right now always matters! In those seasons, the Lord has taught me to long for HIM more than anything else. He has shown me the richness of His provision.

God spoke over me in one of the most tender seasons of my life and showed me that my prayers for removal were the wrong prayers.

I wanted removal, but God wanted renewal.

I don't know why God does what He does, and I don't understand His timetable. Yet, I had to come to this place where I no longer allowed my inability to understand the One who breathed me into existence to cause me to believe for one second that He has some unspoken limitation. I had to come to this place where I didn't allow my inability to understand make me believe that God was somehow powerless to effect change in my life right where He has planted me.

As said at Christ Church Trumbell, "Are you ready to be broken open?"

Every seed that you see on the ground is as alive as the tree or plant next to it. Seeds carry within them a fully alive embryo with all the DNA needed to become the plant it is meant to be. Scientists describe the embryo in seeds as looking much like a person bent over. This embryo is surrounded by nutrients that help the seed germinate. Each seed knows when it is time to unfurl from this bent position. Each seed knows when it is time to stand up and break open its hard shell.

For a seed to achieve its greatest expression, it must come completely undone.

For a seed to achieve its greatest expression, it must come completely undone.

First, the shell cracks. The insides come out. Everything starts to change. To someone who doesn't fully understand growth, it would look like destruction. When we allow God to crack us open and test us in the stretching, deep roots will develop in rich soil. The seed structure may die, but in its place is a tree or plant that stretches up to produce even more seeds.

We need to be broken open in order to be who He has made us to be. To allow ourselves to be broken open to the planting, growing, pruning, and flourishing of the Lord requires vulnerability and trust.

Are we willing to trust God amidst our circumstances?

Are we willing to be whatever He wants us to be?

One must pay the price for fertile soil. We must understand the necessity of allowing Him to be the Master Gardener over our field of soil.

We are not just a single seed. He has put an embryo purpose inside of us. Sometimes breaking open may be painful. But sometimes it is liberating, freeing, and full of hope. Standing up and breaking open that hard shell does not always involve suffering and pain. Sometimes, breaking means tearing down patterns that have served to limit you. Sometimes allowing the seed to die means waking up to the fact that it is time to be who Jesus created you to be. To let go of those things in your life that are holding you back.

Change has the potential to lead us towards deep growth.

In my case, He changed things all right. I wanted Him to change my circumstances. Instead, He began to change me. I wanted Him to move me to a different soil. He wanted to unfurl me so I could encounter my purpose and enrich the soil I was already in.

Perhaps we should stop seeking to be removed from our "Babylon" and instead seek renewal right where we are. I know that's easy to say. It's a whole separate, hard thing to live that out.

Friends, hard and holy things are worth fighting for. They are.

There's a whole hidden world of LIFE happening beneath our feet. Everything a plant will be is already hidden inside of the seed underground!

Everything we need to grow and flourish has already been placed inside us. When we accept Jesus as our Savior, He then lives inside of us. There is now this newly created spiritual soil. Everything we need is already inside us through the seed of Jesus.

God can take the Babylon of your life, even now, and make it a beautiful place for refinement, revival, and restoration. God can take this season that feels like captivity and lead us into a fulfilling, promised land–even if we have to go through the wilderness to get there.

But first, we must surrender our own plans and purposes in exchange for His which are far greater than anything we could cultivate on our own.

You may find yourself in a place or season that you never wanted to be. You may find yourself in the very center of some of the most unfamiliar, unlikely, and undesirable soil. Here is your opportunity to encounter God in a place you never thought He could be found.

REFLECT

- Are you weary today? Take some time to share your burdens with God.
- Are you struggling with where God has "planted" you? Ask Him to help change your perspective and show you significance right where you are.
- Are you in a season or space where you feel misplaced or held captive by people or circumstances around you?
- How can you take small, active steps today to "seek the welfare" of that place, circumstance, or person?
- There is a whole hidden world of life happening underneath the soil that we can't see. How does this encourage you today?

SCRIPTURE

> The Lord will guide you always; He will satisfy your
> needs in a sun-scorched land (exile) and will strengthen
> your frame. You will be like a well-watered garden, like
> a spring whose waters never fail.
>
> Isaiah 58:11

PRAYER

You are the kind of God who is powerful enough that you've planted and placed us in the soil of your Hands. And yet, You are personal enough that You know our name and the very number of hairs on our heads. We desire to be rooted and established. We trust that You have planted us on purpose for a purpose, and that it is not a mistake. Help us to trust that You are doing something we can't see right now. As we place our lives and circumstances in Your Hands, give us strength for this day. We want to be secure through every season's change, withstanding savage winds and scorn. Through You, we can be unshakable. Nurture us in Your Spirit's flow. In Jesus' name, Amen.

CHAPTER THREE

Purpose in Your Placement

Your life may feel like exile right now. You may feel uprooted and misplaced, just like the Israelites. A lot may feel like chaos in this season. When God's will was for the Israelites to be in exile in a foreign place, it wasn't because He forgot about them or because He wanted to destroy or punish them. There was a purpose for that season in their lives.

Gardeners know that there are seasons. In life, there are seasons. Through it all, there are seasons. That can seem really beautiful. Seasons can seem really profound and extravagant and glorious. The adjustments can also feel harsh.

Maybe what we need is more Christians who talk about how hard spiritual growth is.

Letting God change you is hard.

Seeing purpose in painful places is hard.

Staying quiet in spirit when you want to scream is really hard.

Trusting God when you want to freak out is hard.

Holding on when you want to run is hard.

Being in seasons like this doesn't mean that everything is wrong, but it's where we belong.

As I was lying in bed a while back, I was thinking about the seasons of life that I have walked through. It was in this time of reflection that the Lord spoke beauty over my soul.

> **"There has always been a purpose for your placement, sweet child, even and most especially when you couldn't see it or didn't believe it."**

There were many days that I spent begging and pleading with God to get me out of painful seasons. Escape seemed like the quickest solution. I'm sure you've found yourself here, too. I've lived in Babylonian soil. I've encountered harsh realities. For most of my time in exile soil, I cursed it. I spent years being bitter about things I didn't like and things I couldn't control.

You, too, may be in soil right now that feels unfair or unsettling. You may be questioning how God could possibly use this placement for your good.

I know how hard it is to sit in the weight of hardship, to replay disappointments and wonder if you will ever feel joy. When life hits hard, when prayers seem to go unanswered, when you are met with silence instead of solutions, there is a temptation to shrink underneath it all. It can be easy to allow the weight of it to define you.

There have been times in my marriage that were hit some really low spots–pits that the color black didn't even begin to describe. Soil that didn't feel very rich. There were parts in Jeremy and I's stories that were being written differently than either one of us wanted or thought it would be. There were things sacrificed by both of us that felt crushing. Jeremy had to let go of some really valuable things. I had to surrender what I wanted for what felt like a short-ended compromise, not realizing that it was obedience. But God saw us, and He didn't keep us in that captivity forever.

What if this season of soil isn't meant to break you but to build something in you that isn't possible through any other soil?

What if everything that feels like a struggle is making you more rooted?

What if the very things that you wish would go away, are the very things that God is using to make you unshakable?

What if the challenges are proof that He is refining you for a greater purpose?

I am not going to sit here and tell you to push down your emotions. I am not going to sit here and tell you to, "just have faith" as a means to erase your pain. Faith isn't pretending that you are okay when you are not. God doesn't want us to pretend with Him.

Sometimes, you just have to be honest with God, like I was that night. There's no use trying to hide or pretend. Friends, it can be very dangerous if we begin to process our disappointments before others who aren't Him or those who don't know how to lead us back to Him. If our approach to God is in anything other than total transparency and authenticity, we limit the access He has to move in our hearts and lives.

Do you know the really cool thing about God? He doesn't buckle or hold offense when we cry out to him in our pain? He isn't like us in that way. He has broad shoulders. He knows that we can't see all that He can see. His Word says that He weeps with those who weep. He bottles up our tears. He keeps track of all of our sorrows. He doesn't turn away when things get hard. He doesn't abandon us when we don't understand. He doesn't give up on us.

His word in Psalm 23 says that He sets a table before us in the presence of our enemies. He sets the table. He lays all the tableware out. He isn't in a hurry. He isn't dismantled by the hovering of the enemy over our lives. The chatter in our lives doesn't change who God is. He sets before us a feast of His presence in the midst of it! His feast is not a McDonald's bag of fast food. No! He's not about to hurry off. He sets the table. He prepares the feast. He isn't distracted by all the mess heaping around us. He has time for our healing.

He wants us to bring everything to Him. In 1 Peter 5:7, He tells us to cast all of our anxiety on Him because He cares for us. The word "cast" is the Hebrew word "shalach" which means to throw with force. God understands heartache. His desire is not that we would wallow in the worry but that we would throw it on Him.

Do you know why God asks us to throw our anxious thoughts on Him? He knows we will weary in the laboring of our own burdens. God is willing to release us from all that torments our minds.

*We have to decide
that the soil we are
in is where we are
supposed to be.*

This doesn't mean that the hardships will disappear. But it does mean that the hardship won't be wasted. There will be a purpose spring out of the soil because of them. There will be roots that grow down deep because of them. There will be flourishing in bloom because of them.

Friends, we won't live forever in saturated rich soil.

There will be seasons of frustration, exhaustion, pain, nights where questions keep us up in worry. He doesn't want us to stay stuck here. Pain has a way of making us stop moving. It immobilizes us. It makes us stop hoping. It makes us stop believing that things can be different. But real hope–hope in Jesus is choosing to believe that God is still writing your story, even when you can't see the next word.

We have to decide that the soil we are in is where we are supposed to be.

His promises have to carry more weight than our current circumstances. God isn't rushing the process of your healing. He also isn't willing to leave you unhealed. We have to shift our mindset from all that's being lost and taken to all that's being found and given.

God has a future and hope for us even when we suffer in exile or hurt. It is the devil's deception to rob us of the future and hope that God has for us. God had a special purpose in allowing the captivity of his people in Babylon. It was for the preparation of spreading the Gospel. This lengthy captivity revealed God's faithfulness to never leave His people and the assurance of His promises if we trust and follow Him. When the exiles finally returned from captivity, it led to a revival! It birthed a rebuilding! When they surrendered themselves to His rooting, growth began to take place. Even in the deepest seasons, there was purpose for the exiles in captivity.

God has a special purpose for where He has placed us, too. It's so much bigger than us.

Is the easy answer for God to uproot us, reposition us, and place us somewhere else that feels less painful? Is the easy answer for God to send us directly to the Promised Land? Maybe so. But we would be the wrong people when we got there. He loves us more than keeping us in places of comfort. Our placement determines our growth. His desire for us is deep growth.

When we allow our flesh to rule, when we allow how we "feel" in painful seasons of our lives to dictate what we believe about God, it gives us a very distorted view of the goodness of God. We have these faulty thoughts that lead to a deceiving mirror.

Why me?

Why this?

How come for this long?

This isn't what I wanted.

This isn't how I thought it would look.

And so on.

When we do this, we ultimately tell God that we don't trust in the sovereignty of *who* He is.

Have there been parts about seasons of my life that don't feel good? Were there aspects that I wished looked different? Were there areas that I wished I had more control over?

Absolutely.

However, I had to come to terms with the fact that I'm not Alpha and Omega. I don't see it all from beginning to end all at once. I only have flesh eyes that see the right now.

I'm not the Master Gardener. I don't understand the methods required to enrich the soil where I am. I can't see the sovereignty of every plan and how they weave together for my good and my GROWTH!!

I have to *trust the process*, even and most especially when it involves my pain. There is a purpose for *your* placement.

God only gives good.

Even when the season is painful and doesn't look like you thought it would, He's weaving together greatness. Not a granule. Not a droplet. An abundance of good is what He has for us!

I'm so glad that we serve and follow the lead of a God who isn't withholding His goodness from us. He isn't cheating us out of what He has planned.

REFLECT

- What fruitless attempts are you using to try and find meaning in your life right now?
- Are you in a place where you are asking God to remove you from? Church, marriage, workplace, friendship, etc.
- How can you continue to seek the welfare of this place and season today?
- What are some ways that you can choose renewal over removal in your spiritual walk? Ask God to help you grow right where He has planted you this season and trust Him for your growth?

SCRIPTURE

> How abundant are the good things that You have
> stored up for those who live in awe of You.
>
> Psalm 31:19

PRAYER

Heavenly Father, if you are asking me to stay in a place that feels unfair, give me eyes to see what You see. If I am seeking things outside of you for my fulfillment and worth, reveal those things to me. I desire to honor you with my whole life. Show me areas where I am not. When I am in a posture of grumbling and complaining about my circumstances, remind me of the promise that You have for me in Psalm 31. You have a plan to lavish favor over me as I trust You and bless you in front of those watching my life. I also want to bless you in the secret places where no one else sees but me. I place my full confidence in the plan that You have for me, even if I don't understand it all. I trust You. In Jesus' name, amen.

CHAPTER FOUR

Kool-Aid & Tomato Plants

Several years ago, when my boys were both much younger (babies really), the three of us loaded up into our minivan and headed down the road about 8 miles to take my youngest, at the time, to the doctor. Case had been experiencing excruciating ear pain, and I was certain that he had an ear infection that needed medication. While on our way, I noticed that the gas light was on. I quickly sighed as I remembered that I had tucked my last $10 bill in the side section of my purse. My plan was to put that $10 of gas in the van and head straight for the doctor's office.

As Case was screaming in the back seat, our eldest son, Hunter, said, "Mom, if I'm good while we wait at the doctor, can I get a cheap toy after?" My heart tightened up almost instantly. I knew there wasn't money for it. Unlike God, our supplies are not endless. They run out. This particular day, my supply had run entirely out.

"No, buddy. I only have $10 and I'm using that money to fill the van up with gas because we are miles away from running out of gas."

He took the response pretty well for a 4-year-old, but I could see the gears turning in his mind. He quickly replied, "Don't you say that you buy Kool-Aid for us to drink because it's cheap? Why can't you just put Kool-Aid in the van for gas?"

I still, to this day, can remember internally laughing at the thought of that. To him, it made perfect sense. I pondered that conversation for several days. God revealed to me that so many of us are just like that.

Now you know how ridiculous it would seem if someone told you that they were going to put Kool-Aid in their gas tank for their vehicle to run. It would never work. But here's the thing, unlike Kool-Aid in my vehicle, many of us use the variables we do to try and gain fulfillment from the emptiness in our soul because it IS effective for a little while. However, it never fully satisfies. It still leaves us searching, which is why the hurt never lets up. We are continuously searching. It's why the feelings of loneliness never fully vanish.

One of the most detrimental shakings in my early walk with the Lord was rooted in insecurity, which led to longings for the wrong things. There were a multitude of fruitless attempts to find meaning. My root system was all wrong. It was shallow. It was withering. It was rotting beneath the surface. (We will talk more about root systems later on. Root systems are a big deal for our growth.)

If there is an award for the woman who has made the most attempts in searches for fulfillment, I think I'd be holding the biggest trophy, wearing the biggest crown, and standing on the highest pedestal. That takes a lot of humility to share. It's not something I'm proud of, but something that I think needs to be shared. Vulnerability is what opens the door to healing after all. This is my healing story, and I pray that this book tills up the hard soil of your heart so that you can allow God to heal you, too.

When we see our reflection, we more than likely focus on the flaws, the imperfections, the mistakes, the shortcomings, the failures. Our reflection becomes a weighty burden of all the regrets and changes we wish we could make. It is imperative that we know that is not how God sees us. Not even close. I know that when I have had really bad days and made really bad choices, the enemy convinces me that that is also all that God sees when He looks at me: a series of mess-ups and disappointments.

While God may see our mistakes, our sins, and our weaknesses, He sees past every single one of them and sees the lavishing love that He has for us!

We spent a few years living in a town called Pella, Iowa, while I was finishing my college degree. Every spring, Pella holds a huge event called Tulip Time, where people from all over the world come to take pictures of the gorgeous display of tulips that the community has planted throughout the town. I had never seen anything like it. Hundreds…and I mean hundreds of people scatter the town and courthouse lawn to take pictures and videos in front of these displays. It's incredible!

I'm a gardener. I love nurturing my flower beds and garden areas. Naturally, the Lord speaks to me, oftentimes, through metaphors as I look after my produce and flowers. There was this one singular moment that emerged very early on in my Babylon season and led to an ongoing chatter in my life for a lot of years: "You're not significant."

It was the moment I realized I was just a tomato plant. What I mean by this is this: Tomato plants are full of abundant fruit. They provide a lot of produce over the course of several months. They bring sustainment and nourishment. They have a lot of amazing and vital characteristics and traits for the benefit of so many. They are versatile–many eat from them in different forms!

But people aren't captivated by tomato plants. Tomato plants don't stop traffic. People don't get in line to take pictures in front of them. They just don't. When was the last time you saw someone bent over with their rump up in the air, trying to get the perfect angle of a tomato plant with their camera or phone?

People just aren't captivated by tomato plants.

There was this moment when I allowed myself to believe, metaphorically, of course, that that's what I was. A tomato plant that captivated no one.

It was at that same moment that I felt cheated.

What if I would be more fulfilled as a tulip (or anything else for that matter)?

What if I wanted to be what I could choose?

What if something more stunning would bring more satisfaction and recognition?

This area of my life was something that I had to surrender to the Lord daily–oftentimes, multiple times a day. There was a very early infestation of pollution in the soil of my heart that made everything skewed. That infestation that I allowed to germinate and bring forth corruption led to a rippling of jealousy and envy. I knew He had given me gifts and talents, but they didn't seem as remarkable as the gifts and talents that I saw in those around me. They didn't seem as impressive. I coveted the giftings of people in my midst. I thought I would feel more fulfilled if I had what they had.

My placement not only felt painful, but who He created me to be in that particular soil felt equally unsatisfying, saddening and undesirable.

When we live inside the envelope of this type of wrong security, self-centeredness, and deceit, it chokes the roots of everything that God is growing. It breeds pesticides into our soil.

Years ago, I nicknamed the enemy in my life a "chatterbox." He's always got something to say. There's never a time when he's not talking. His words aren't true, but they are loud. It's amazing how much we allow ourselves to believe when what's being said is loud and frequent. Believing those lies truly is the ultimate insult to God. When we comment on how deficient we are, it says a lot about what we think of God's ability.

Moses is one of my favorite characters in the Bible, and I think it's because I see so much of him in me.

We can learn so much from Moses. God had powerful assignments for Moses. Moses, in all of his insecurity and feelings of inadequacy, answered God's call on His life with this question, "Who am I?" Who am I to be used by you? Who am I?!" Moses even tried negotiating with God by begging God to send someone else out to complete the assignment. "Send someone else to the soil." In this, he is willing to forfeit being the very vessel God desires to use due to his own insecurities.

The driving force behind it all was insecurity and a lack of trust in God's ability. It was rooted in all the wrong things. It was rooted in man. It was rooted in pride. It was rooted in self-dependency. It was rooted in doubt, fear, and disbelief. It was rooted in a lack of trust. You can see it in Moses' hesitancy to obey God.

In my early walk with the Lord, there were a lot of assignments that I knew I was disobedient in stepping into because of my inability to believe that I had much to offer. I couldn't see how God could turn my little into much. I thought someone else would do it better. In my desire for different giftings, I missed a multitude of opportunities to be used through the gifts I did possess. There was hesitancy for me to obey God, the same as there was for Moses.

God's response to Moses in Exodus 4:11-16 is the same paraphrased response He STILL gives to us today:

"Is it not I, it is the Lord who…"

Fill in that blank!

He is the one who fulfills every longing.
He is the one who brings power to all of our weaknesses.
He is the one who offers worth, identity, and security.
He is the one who satisfies every craving.
He is the one who uses every deficiency to infuse His power!
He is the one who goes before us in every assignment!
He is the One who will till and prepare the soil!
He is the One!

Psalm 107:8 says, **He satisfies the longing soul.**

Only God can satisfy the deepest desires of our hearts. Many of us have gone after things and people to satisfy, only to discover that the voids we have still remain. God has so much more to fill and fuel us than the cheap measures we use. He isn't a God that short-changes us. He isn't that way.

The Voice we listen to and believe, will determine the future we experience. As soon as God starts telling you what He wants to do through you, the enemy will use your history to inform any wrong security you have. He will try to derail you through the spirit of error. He will bring before you lie after lie to disrupt God's destiny for you.

God sees every bit of our potential. He DESIGNED our purpose. He knew of every flaw, mistake, and weakness long before we did, and He loves us anyway. He loves you anyway! Lean into the way God sees you. You are created exactly the way He wanted you to be.

the voice we listen to and believe, will determine the future we experience.

REFLECT

- What cheap measures ("Koolaid") are you using to fill your spiritual tank?
- In your insecurities, have you desired different giftings from the Lord?

Identify areas where putting your security in the wrong things is choking out the ways that God wants to use you. Surrender these to the Lord today, and ask Him to help you see yourself the way that He sees you.

SCRIPTURE

> I praise You because I am fearfully and wonderfully made; Your works are beautiful, I know that full well.
>
> Psalm 139:14

PRAYER

Heavenly Father, Your Word says that I am fearfully and wonderfully made. You say that You have good plans for my life. Help me to surrender what I want now for what I want most. I trust that You have created me exactly how you desired for me to be. You have knit me together with pleasure and purpose. Any chatter that comes against these truths are not from You. Help me to lean into Your promise for my life and for my future, so that I can live a life of joy and hope. Bless me so that I can be a blessing to others. In Jesus' name, Amen.

CHAPTER FIVE
I'll Have What He's Having

During one of the most demanding seasons of motherhood, against my better judgment, I allowed my middle child, Case, to pack his own school lunch. With a smile on his face, he did! He was a toothless 5-year-old with a grin that could make everything feel right in the world. He just had that way about him and still does! That very charisma is what led me to cave.

It felt like one of those moments that seemed a little too good to be true. If you've been a mom for very long, you know that there is something to be said for that mom instinct. It's usually pretty spot-on. The mom in me decided to double-check the inside of his lunch box before he left for school. What I found was both hysterical and appalling.

Forty-eight pieces of bubble gum. That's right, I counted.

"Really, Case?

"But that's what I wanted for lunch."

"I understand, son. *But it's not what you need.*"

That statement alone should send us into layers of self-reflection.

As I watched him walk into the school doors with a re-packed lunch, my mind replayed our previous conversation.

Almost immediately, God brought me to Philippians 4:19.

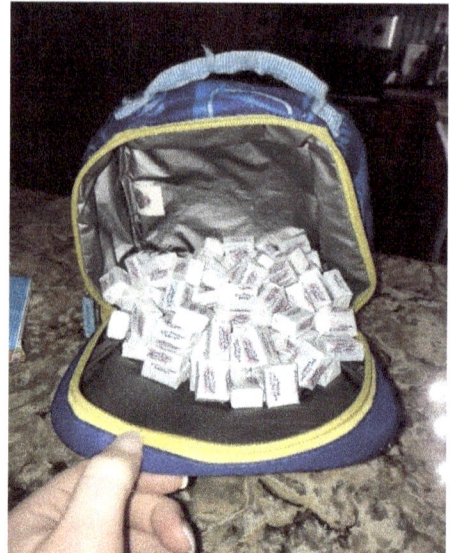

> God will meet all your needs according to
> His glorious riches in Christ Jesus.
> Philippians 4:19

It doesn't state that God will fulfill all of our wants. No! Thank goodness for that. There have been and continue to be moments in my life where what I think I want is not what He knows I need. His Word declares that He will meet all of our needs. Only He knows what it is that our hearts, minds and souls need in order to truly be fulfilled so that we can grow and flourish. Looking back over my life, I'm thankful for so many things that I prayed that He didn't give me.

As I've been on my journey with Jesus, I am slowly learning how unfair it has been of me to judge God's love for me based on what I want Him to give me rather than what He knows that I need.

Later on, we will talk more about the necessity for a plant to have water, for us to have living water. Briefly, I'll note here that water is the agent that allows for the plant's growth. It's natural for us to want sunny days where we are basking under the warmth of comfort. However, God knows that if rain never comes, we won't grow and mature as we should. Rain is a vital agent of growth.

Planting seeds inevitably changes how I feel about rain.

He is sovereign. He knows all things. His thoughts are higher than ours. I have found this to be true over and over again in my life. When my gaze is fixed on Him alone, the desires of my heart transform, change, and begin to align with what brings Him glory.

> Delight yourself in the Lord and
> He will give you the desires of your heart.
> Psalm 37:4

This scripture has become a staple in my life throughout my spiritual journey. So often, we have this truth backward. We want God to give us what we want, and THEN we will delight in Him. Do you know the problem with that? We can't know what's best for us without delighting in Him. We won't accept what He gives if we aren't delighting in Him—especially when it looks different than what we thought it would.

Sometimes, it is undesirable soil that we need, and if we aren't delighting in Him, we will begin cursing the very ground in which God intended us to flourish.

We can't possibly fathom the abundance of all that He has for us if we aren't finding ourselves in a posture of delight with Him. Delighting ourselves in Him doesn't mean we must understand it all. It doesn't mean that we even have to like it all, or any of it, for that matter. Delighting ourselves in Him just means that He becomes our focus rather than the circumstances we see. He becomes our gaze more than all else.

Sometimes, the commentary of our lives is no better than the circumstances we are going through. Friends, I have lived that travesty. There is what I want, and then there's where I'm at. That chasm, when fixated upon, can be unbearably frustrating. This stronghold that becomes impregnated causes us to accept people, spaces, and circumstances as unchangeable. That type of mindset can lead to such hopelessness. We accept life "as is" and live forever in the lack of all that He has for us. We can become complacent in the tolerance of all that we know.

Sometimes it is undesirable soil that we need, and if we aren't delighting in Him, we will begin cursing the very ground in which God intended us to flourish.

When our oldest son was nine years old, he heard about DiGiorno pizza.

He wanted to try it so badly. He begged for weeks for us to buy one for him to try. My husband and I decided to surprise him one evening and cook two DiGiorno pizzas for supper. In typical mom fashion, I was multitasking and totally forgot about the pizza on the bottom rack. The result? A black bottom pizza. I felt horrible. Hunter had been looking forward to this pizza for weeks. Sacrificially, Jeremy and I decided that we would eat the burnt pizza and give the boys the perfectly cooked pizza.

After he and Case had consumed the entire first pizza, Hunter said, "Can I have some more pizza?" I responded with, "Well, the other pizza is burnt to a crisp on the bottom, but you can have some if you'd like."

After a few bites, he wrinkled his little nine-year-old nose and said, "How did you guys even eat that?! It's awful."

My response was easy. "That's all we know. We didn't taste how good the non-burnt pizza was. So, to us, this isn't so bad."

As I was inwardly laughing and replaying our conversation over that burnt pizza, I couldn't help but think about how that is US! How often are we content with shallow roots in our relationship with Christ because it is all we know? Yet, we still have this longing for fulfillment that the world couldn't begin to fill.

How often are we completely and utterly content to continue our lives like so because it's all we've ever known? Are we missing out on experiencing abundant growth through deeper roots? Outwardly, we may look pleasing and acceptable, but what lies beneath the surface isn't really all that impressive.

How often are we eating blackened, burnt pizza, having no idea the greatness and abundant joy that is waiting for us?

A co-worker whom we have coined as the "world traveler" had just gotten back from one of her most recent trips. Upon return, I asked her to catch me up on all her trip highlights. I asked all of the vital vacation questions:

What sightseeing did you do?

How was the weather?

Where did you eat?

What was the funnest experience you had?

What opportunities did God give you to share the gospel?

All the essential follow-up vacation topics. We circled back to the "where did you eat?" She shared an incredible story with me that I knew needed to be grafted into this book. It's one of those things that are simple yet holds so much profound truth.

> "Mom and I were at Chili's, and I had ordered little quesadilla bites–which normally I don't get, but I wanted to switch things up a bit. The waiter accidentally brought me cheeseburger bites instead. He realized that he brought me the wrong thing and eventually brought me the right order of quesadilla bites. I ended up receiving both the quesadillas that I originally wanted, as well as the cheeseburger bites–which were an accident.
>
> It had been right after this event where I felt like I had misheard God's voice or had been led to a dead end in my road at the time.
>
> Oddly enough, I ended up liking the cheeseburger bites way better than my order of quesadillas. Even more oddly, I felt huge comfort in knowing that sometimes we want quesadillas so badly and want to make that order work, but God has these cheeseburgers meant for us. It may not make sense when we get the wrong meal order or get stuck at a dead end, but in the long run, God knows our tastes, our needs, and our story."

How many times have you prayed for God to do something, and when He "brings the order out," it looks drastically different from what you ordered from Him?

I don't want Him to send me what I ordered when the platter that He has for me is so much better!

Throw my order out!

Let's have what He's having.

Let's find purpose in where He has planted us...even now–right here!

He has plans of greatness pouring down over us. And yes—sometimes that means walking through seasons that require deep faith, radical obedience, and the dying of flesh. Sometimes, it feels like rain. We must get to a place where we don't oppose the stormy, rainy days. They hold purpose. They are part of what He has for us to grow us.

Let's be real...

Sometimes the desires of our hearts look about as childish and ridiculous as forty-eight pieces of bubble gum for lunch. Sometimes, the desires of our hearts are frustrated when the little cheeseburgers come out on a platter, and we anticipate something different.

God loves you. He loves you so much to withhold what you think you want from you. He promises to give you what you need as it aligns with the beautiful plan He has paved out for you.

Take delight in Him.

Praise Him where you've been planted.

You will begin to see the desires of your heart change. And that, my friend, is perhaps the most beautiful thing of all.

REFLECT

- Just like plants need rain to be nourished and to grow, stormy days are necessary for our growth, too. How does this give you perseverance in the disappointing days?
- God is not withholding anything good from you! Is it time to toss your order out so that you can receive the abundant platter that God has for you? Is it time to trade out those 48 pieces of bubble gum, black-bottomed pizza, and quesadilla bites so that you can experience all that He has for you?
- Psalm 37 promises that if we delight ourselves in Him, He will give us the desires of our hearts. How can you be intentional today about delighting yourself in Him?

SCRIPTURE

> The Lord God is our sun and shield. He gives us grace and glory. The Lord will not hold back anything good from those who walk uprightly with Him.
>
> Psalm 84:11

PRAYER

Declare this today: Lord, I trust what You are doing. I will cling to Your truth. I trust what You have ordered for me! A mouthful of forty-eight pieces of bubble gum is just a mouthful of nothing! You have more for me! Only Your Divine Hand knows the why behind it all. Help me to keep my mind parked not on the "why" but on the "WHO" that understands all of the whys. I love you, Lord. I trust and follow Your lead. I choose to take delight in You today and accept that the stormy and rainy days hold purpose. Help me to grow in You. In Jesus' name, amen.

*You say I'm called to be
An Oak of Righteousness.
But how can I possibly rise
From the remnants of this dust?*

*There's only darkness here,
Just underneath the soil.
I just want to escape this,
So, I labor and I toil.*

*I fight against this place,
This barren, captive land
I feel like you've forgotten me,
It's so hard to see your hand.*

*Surrender to the soil,
Though full of thistle and of weeds.
Make a home in this place,
That you never wanted to be.*

*A seed can't escape,
And yet expect to grow.
There's a purpose in your placement,
So hold tight to Him who knows.*

*This place where I am planted,
May you do your deepest work.
Renewing every part of me,
By the power of your Word.*

PART TWO

To undergo development by increasing in size & changing physically;
progress to maturity.

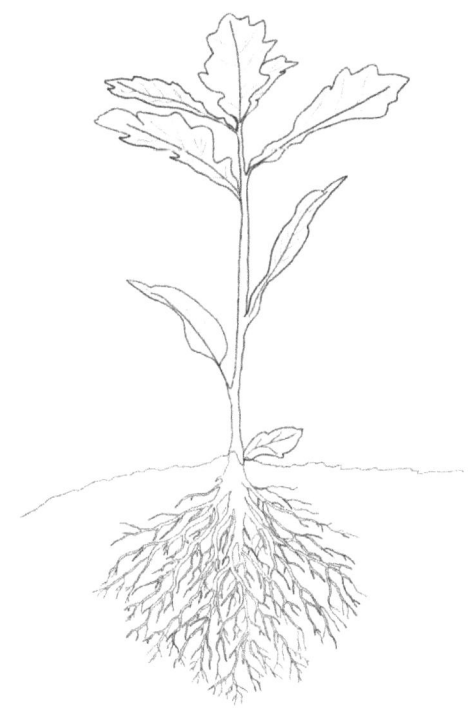

CHAPTER SIX

Preparing the Soil

Each year when it is time to prepare my garden for the next season, I see a path that has been tread on year after year, leaving the soil compacted. Parts of our hearts can be hard, like that path, leaving what falls there to be exposed. If there is one thing that I'm learning about myself, it's this: When the seed of God's word falls on my hardened heart, it is unresponsive to the work of the Master Gardener.

Our hearts are the hub of our personality. It is from the overflow of our hearts, that we say and do. What comes out of our mouths begins in our hearts. What actions we take are birthed from the nucleus of our hearts.

> It is from the overflow of our hearts, that our mouths speak.
> Luke 6:45

What sprouts up from underneath is largely due to the nature of the soil. When I hear my kids say something hateful, spiteful, or rude, I used to respond like this: "That's not the way we should talk." But God is showing me that my response is addressing only the behavior. It's just an attempt at behavior modification, and a poor one at that. Anyone can modify their behavior temporarily for a certain time, space, or setting. Anyone can do that.

My daughter, Hattie Pearl, has loved makeup since before she could walk. She's seven now, and she knows more about application and contouring than I do. We went through a phase where she would wake up in the mornings for school and immediately put her lipstick on. I would try to explain to her that her approach to the morning routine was backward–that she needed to brush her teeth first. She continually insisted that "it was fine. People will see my pretty lipstick and won't care if I've brushed my teeth or not."

It took my persistence and discipline to explain to her that at some point throughout the day, she would open her mouth, and when she opened it, people would smell the stench of what she didn't clean up. At that point, there are not enough layers of lipstick to cover up the stink.

Isn't that so true for us in our lives and the lives of those around us? There isn't enough outward adornment to cover up the rotting within. I want to go deeper with my kids. I want deeper growth for them than just ironed clothes and polished words on Sunday morning. I want to lead them to deeper growth. Now, when they spout something off that is clothed in a garment of malice or anger, I have begun saying things like this: "What is bothering you? What are you thinking about? How are you hurting?" Because more than behavior modification, I want heart transformation.

I want them to receive a spiritual heart transplant.

After all, isn't that really what we all need?

One of my favorite heart transplant stories in the Bible is found in the fifth Chapter of John. There's this man who has been paralyzed for 38 years and is lying by a pool called Bethesda. He is on his mat, a thin mattress that the poor people would use for bedding. I believe it became his place of comfort. You don't lay on a mat for 38 years and not have butt imprints. That mat was defining for him in immeasurable ways. It held everything about him.

This is one of my favorite stories of healing in the Bible because it speaks of paralysis. Paralysis doesn't have to be just a handicap to the body. Paralysis can handicap a person's mind. It can immobilize every single thing that God has for you and leave you in bondage to the enemy and every desire he has to steal, kill, and destroy the will of God for your life. This type of paralysis can be just as destructive to a person's spiritual growth as nearly anything else. That was me. I was paralyzed by every taunt of the enemy over my life through wrong identity and inadequacies:

You'll never fit in.
You're too unique.
You're too different.
You're not special enough.
You don't have the right talents.
The gifts you have aren't extraordinary.
No one even notices you.

You're not enough.

The taunting of the enemy made me strive to become someone different, yet there was this reality that no amount of striving would ever be enough. It stifled my growth. It handicapped every dream, vision, and purpose. While I was not physically paralyzed, my mind and heart were.

This type of paralysis can leave a person feeling completely helpless. In this man's case, the waters that could heal him were nearby, but he couldn't get to them. The thing he thought could heal him — and he badly needed healing — felt far off. He couldn't reach it. He couldn't get there. He was cut off from the source of healing, and utterly paralyzed. What's more, he was cut off from the people around him, too, as he competed with the crowd to be the first to get into the pool when the waters bubbled up. No one knows fully what he was feeling, but I imagine anxiety, frustration, desperation, even despair — all those painful, negative feelings that are stirred up when we feel helpless, vulnerable, and alone.

Those circumstances are the perfect ingredients for a hardened heart.

We can feel paralyzed by grief, paralyzed by doubt or indecision, paralyzed by hurt and betrayal. Like that man beside the pool, we can feel completely immobilized. Like him, we can feel alone in the crowd, utterly deprived of anyone to help.

We are about to embark upon the most precious and pivotal moment of this story.

> When Jesus saw the man lying there and knew that he had been there a long time, he said to him, 'Do you want to be made well?'

My first time reading this story, that question caught me off guard. Of course, he wanted to be made well! Why did Jesus even ask that?! Jesus could take one look at the situation, pick the man up without a word, and carry him straight to the pool of healing water. Why waste time? Why bother asking such an obvious question?

The Greek word for "made well" is "hugies," which means sound, whole, complete. Jesus is referring to a deeper work than simply healing this man's body of paralysis. He wanted to heal his mind, too. The word "made well" in its original language actually refers to mind, body, and soul. It extends beyond physical well-being.

Jesus didn't ask the man if he wanted to feel better. He asked Him if He wanted to get well.

We can come to church and feel better, but not get well.

We can talk to a bunch of people and share our burdens and feel better, but not get well.

Jesus' question reveals something important about God. The God we meet in Jesus will never force or push, even when it comes to offering healing. Jesus deeply respects our freedom and gives us the option to choose. Do we want the grace and healing that God is offering us? Will we give our consent? It is not just a rhetorical question. The question invites the man beside the pool — and invites us, as well — to explore and examine what we truly want and why. There's power in admitting that we aren't well. It's what offers the tilling Hand of the Gardener to begin working up the hardened soil.

Do we really want to be made well? That's the question.

I've stood in front of this very question multiple times in my life. In some seasons, the answer sometimes isn't a clean-cut one. Sometimes, the answer looks like this: "Jesus, I'm hurting. I've been paralyzed by this heart wound for a long time. Some part of me feels comfortable playing the role of the innocent victim. Some part of me feels justified in blaming the other person for wounding or offending me or for keeping me buried underneath the most undesirable soil."

Staying stuck is the easier option. It requires less work. Laying on a mat for 38 years and cursing everything and everyone around you is easier than singing a song of worship when you can't see or understand anything that God could possibly be doing for your good in that season of paralysis.

Staying buried removes us from repairing what we allowed someone else to destroy.

I believe we have created this habit of grumbling and complaining. We look for excuses, so much so, that it quickly becomes the loudest narrative in our story. Why me? I could have been fully alive and well — but then I got hurt, and I stopped trusting God. So here I am, buried underneath this cursed soil, stuck forever on the very edge of healing, with healing so close but never quite possible.

When Jesus asks the paralyzed man by the pool if he wants to be made well, the man's response is a mess of an answer. He responds with blame and complaint.

> I have no one to put me into the pool when the water is stirred up; and while I am making my way, someone else steps down ahead of me.

You'll notice that the loudest narrative was focused on self. He was surrounded by a multitude of people who also needed healing. His anger is that he isn't being healed. Sometimes, it feels like that in our lives, doesn't it? It can feel like everyone around us is getting a hand-up and a handout. We can feel overlooked and forgotten about, like that little seed that is buried underneath the darkest soil.

This man had been waiting a long time to get to the water for healing. In fact, many of his excuses were wrapped up in the truth that everybody else was getting to the water before him. We are taught that the first one wins. The first one gets it all. But the grace of God says, let the last be first. Let the one who has waited receive it all.

Those of you begging God for a breakthrough, you don't have to beg Him for what He already did for you through the finished work of Jesus. When God decides to do a work in your life, it's done if you will give your consent and surrender your life to Him.

Jesus responds pretty straightforwardly to the paralyzed man. "Stand up, take up your mat and walk." At once, the man was made well. Healing isn't far off. It's not made available to only the elite. This man was a nobody with nothing to offer Jesus. Healing is available for us through the God we meet in Jesus. But we have to want it. Opening the door to growth requires honest self-examination. We have to know we need it.

I want to experience the fullness of life, to experience freedom, to encounter the vibrancy of life outside of this paralysis—without holding back. The Gospel does not record that conversation, but I imagine this sick man looked up at Jesus and made that consensual first step towards inviting Jesus to do some deep healing work and free him from his bondage.

Healing is not a one-time occurrence most times. Oftentimes, it is a process. We see that in this man's story. When studying this passage with my husband, he pointed out something really profound. The same man that Jesus healed in verse 8 is now tripped up again in verse 14, when Jesus pursues him yet again. Healing is a process. But Jesus is always pursuing us so that our healing can be complete.

All of you gardeners know that the deep work is the hard work. It doesn't matter how long it takes, how painful the change is, how confused you are or how lonely it will be. This is the path of growth you need to take, until one day, you'll look back and thank yourself for not giving up.

The preparation work usually involves tools: a tiller, a shovel and work gloves. It's not a glamorous job and it won't be easy. This is the portion of the book where I beg you to dig deep and discover the bedrock of what you really want. Sift out and sort through all the lesser wants. Deep down, we should all want our lives to  be about something so much larger than ourselves and our endless striving and self-promotion. Discover what it is that will bring you to a place of freedom and lead you into the pathway of spiritual growth and maturity. It's a process.

When it comes to healing, Jesus does not appear out of nowhere, waving a magic wand. What Jesus asks is more demanding than that and more costly. Jesus tells the man that He just healed to stop sinning. He knows that the greater healing for this man is to live in freedom. It is our greatest healing, too. He needs us to partner with Him in doing the work. The degree to which you want to be made well is the degree to which you

God desires to till up the soil of your heart and make it soft again.

will choose to do this deep work of healing with Him so that you can grow in all that He has for you.

When I think of the paralyzed man at the pool who had been in this condition for 38 years, there's no way that he wasn't also suffering from a hardened heart. His mat was the very place that caused him so much disdain. It was the reminder of everything that felt so crippling. It was the place where he, too, felt buried underneath undesirable soil. He'd been there a long time. I can resonate with that. Days feel like years.

It's hard to stay in a place where you don't want to be…under the weight and uncertainty of ever being free.

I'm sure that if we came alongside and sat down next to him on his mat near the pool, we would hear a story of abandonment, hurt, disdain, pain, betrayal, frustration, anger, bitterness, and resentment. The list could go on and on.

A hardened heart is not the initial suffering. It's the response to something that happened first. It's just the response. It's the effect. It's the echo back to our pain. The enemy loves for our pain and our hardened hearts to keep in close communication. The more they hold hands, the more in bondage we become. The harder our hearts become, the more in pain we are. This cycle is detrimental to our spiritual growth. It's detrimental to how we live and love.

You will notice that the man did not need to climb into the healing pool to be healed. The healing spring was not outside him but inside of him, through the power of Jesus. In the center of my deepest pain and heartache, I prayed for removal. I begged God to rescue me out of the soil. To reposition me. To plant me again somewhere else. I prayed for him to bring me new circumstances. But the healing power wasn't outside of me. It was inside of me–through Jesus.

Your circumstances changing isn't the thing that will soften your heart. You can find yourself in a renewed set of circumstances and may still carry your hardened heart into that space, too.

People changing how they treat you will not be the component that will bring healing and growth. They can change, and you can find yourself in a renewed space with them, and there will be somebody else who will come along and wound you again.

If your heart is sick, every new soil will become polluted. You can have everything around you change, and it won't fix a hardened heart. The healing spring is not outside of you. It's inside of you–through the power of Jesus. There are a multitude of things that can cause a hardened heart.

- Trauma
- Abandonment
- Arrogance & Pride
- Legalism (striving to earn blessings from God and others)
- Disappointments
- Betrayal
- Physical/Emotional/Mental pain as a result from tragedy or loss
- Sin

Take a few minutes to read through that list again. Which ones apply to you?

There are some really easy indicators that will further reveal whether you are experiencing the effects of a hardened heart in your life. Indicators are the gauge that shows the state or level of something. It's easy for us to be in denial about things in our lives that we've been carrying for a long time. We get used to the weight and don't even realize it's there anymore.

Here is your opportunity for you to be real with yourself and with God. Read through the list below and take some time for inner reflection.

INDICATORS THAT YOU MAY HAVE A HARDENED HEART:

- ☐ Suffering from feelings of bitterness/resentment
- ☐ Inability to worship or thank God
- ☐ Critical spirit
- ☐ Isolating yourself from God & others
- ☐ Refusal to forgive
- ☐ Pride
- ☐ Lacking in compassion
- ☐ Refusal to serve others
- ☐ Refusal to be ministered to

When God's word and truth fall onto the soil of a hardened heart, it is less likely to settle into deep places and produce change in us. In fact, I'd venture to say that when the seed of God's word falls on a hardened heart, it gets blown away by the winds of life or plucked away by the enemy before it ever has a chance to get planted into our hearts.

Operating with a hardened heart in our spiritual walk hinders personal growth through Jesus. We will talk more about that throughout this segment. For now, I'd like you to read through the following characteristics of a hardened heart below and take time to transparently check the characteristics that are real for you today.

CHARACTERISTICS OF A HARDENED HEART:

- ☐ Inability to see from His perspective
- ☐ Disinterested in hearing God's voice which leads to lacking in wisdom & understanding
- ☐ Failure to remember all that God has done & how He has delivered
- ☐ Disobedience
- ☐ Unrepentance
- ☐ Lacking expectancy for what God can do
- ☐ Unbelief

Tackling the rotting and shallow root issues is not an easy task, but it's rewarding.

How do we prepare the field of our heart for the seeds that He wants to plant and grow in us?

I believe the answer is by asking Him to till the soil of this hard space.

Put your spiritual work gloves on, grab the shovel, and get in there with Him. Dig deep and do the hard work towards growth and maturation.

God desires to till up the soil of your heart and make it soft again.

He has time.

I would venture to say that no step of growth matters more than this one!

Years back, when my oldest son, Hunter, was only about 6, and his younger brother, Case, was around 3, they were in their bedroom playing with toys. It was time for us to shift our day and head to town, so I instructed them to take a few minutes to pick up their mess. The conversation that soon followed between the two of them was so profound that I had to document it:

Hunt: Case, you have to help clean up the toy room with me.

Case: No.

Hunt: You got toys out, too. That means you have to clean them up with me.

Case: No.

Hunt: Then you better not play with toys anymore if you can't learn to pick them up.

It was at this point that Case chose to whop Hunter in the back of the head with a rubber snake.

After about 15 minutes of trying to make Case apologize and him refusing, I walked away to hear this:

Hunt: "You don't have to be sorry for what you did, Case. I'm gonna forgive you anyway."

How can two short sentences be so powerful? These words settled deep into the very soil of my heart.

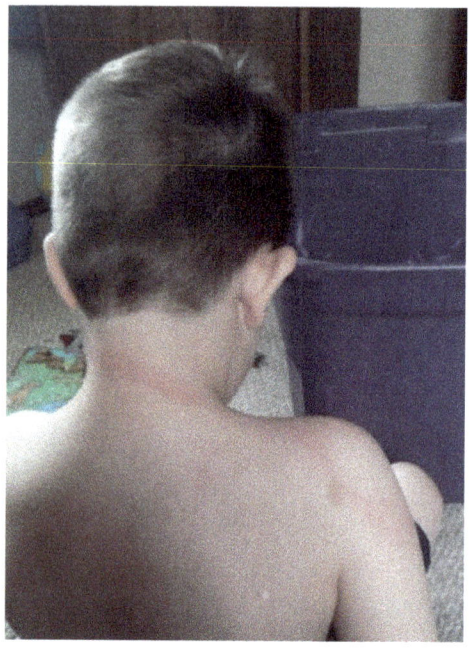

Sometimes, it feels like we've been slapped in the back of the head by a rubber snake, too— by circumstances or people we didn't expect, and in ways that we didn't see coming. It can come out of nowhere and leave us suffering. The enemy makes us believe that that pathway to feeling free is spending all our time chasing down the snake that bit us to ask why it did. But all that does is keep us bitterly bound.

There are times when the mess we are asked to clean up isn't entirely all our own. Some of it may be. In our humanness, we feel more justified when those who have wreaked havoc in our lives own up to it and step in to help clean up the mess they've made. But that's just not how it usually works. Oftentimes, it looks nothing like that.

More often than not, it looks exactly like that picture I just portrayed for you.

The mess you are staring at today may have these names: hurt, pain, betrayal, abandonment, loss, or grief. And that's exactly what it is, a mess. It's all you see. It affects everything about you. You have to sidestep around it every single day, just to function. It's surrounding you! There may be no one BUT GOD willing to pick it all up. God wants to be the gardener of your soul today. He has time. He wants to be the one who cares for your soil. He has time for your healing.

For those drowning in bitterness and unforgiveness, there is power in recognizing that God knows, and that's enough. God knows what's been stolen from you. He sees the heartache you are under. He knows what has happened. Jesus runs after the ones who are shattered and broken. If you are bound in bitterness and unforgiveness, He is running after you to heal you, to restore all that's been taken, and to redeem every piece of it.

He has time for your healing.

You may not need more therapy to forgive those who hurt you. You might just need a deeper realization of Jesus. The greater the revelation of His worth, the greater our desire to forgive. We recall the cost paid to erase every debt. Holding onto unforgiveness is telling Jesus that His blood on the cross wasn't enough. When we forgive, we are also announcing that Jesus is worthy. His glory far surpasses any offense. It is a testament that we believe that He is worthy.

Healing begins the minute you surrender it all into His hands and His care as the Master Gardener of your soil.

Let Him deposit seeds of grace, mercy, and forgiveness over you today. This was the first step for me in my spiritual journey with Jesus. My heart was very hard–like concrete. I could have checked every single box above. Every single one. I needed a spiritual heart transplant. I desperately needed Him to work the hard soil. I needed Him to till and uproot some things that had been planted on the soil of my heart and mind from the enemy. There were things that had settled that were wreaking havoc.

We need His word and truth to settle into our hearts in a way that will lead to growth.

It is imperative that the soil of our hearts stay soft for Him.

REFLECT

- Like soil, our hearts can be cultivated and improved. How does this encourage you to know that He is partnering with you in preparing the soil?
- Ask the Holy Spirit to help search your thoughts and ponder these factors above that you have checked. Consider what areas of your life may be hardened and unworked like the path described. This is an important first step towards growth.
- What are some areas of your life that you need to revisit and spend some time asking God to heal? Healing is a process in the growth journey. Take some time with Jesus near this spiritual pool and tell Him how you would like to be made well.
- How does it make you feel to know that God desires to give you a new heart?

SCRIPTURE

> I will give you a new heart and put a new spirit in you; I will remove from you your heart of stone and give you a heart of flesh.
>
> Ezekiel 36:26

PRAYER

Father God, along the way, I have picked up some baggage because of my experiences. I ask you to root out my heart's bitterness, unforgiveness, hardness, hurt, pain, unbelief, distrust, and every unfruitful battle wound, and doubt and replace it with a new heart. You are Jehovah Raphe–the God who heals. I am inviting you in to heal the hardened spaces in my heart. Work up the soil. Soften my heart so that I can love like You. You alone know the many ways I've been hurt. You see the hardened places in my heart that affect how I grow and love. I desire to receive whatever it is You are planting within me in this next season. Remove anything that will spoil the vineyard. I trust You with it all and want to be made well. I pray that Your Word will not be wasted on me. In Jesus' name, Amen.

CHAPTER SEVEN
Seeds That Get Snatched

A wise farmer carefully cultivates the soil before his spring planting. In the same way, God has been preparing the soil of your heart for this moment on your spiritual journey.

I love the picture of God being the Master Gardener in my life.

Jesus provides essential elements for our growth. He gives us His Word (the Bible) for fertilizer over the soil of our hearts and minds. His fertilizer is stirred into the soil of our hearts and minds to produce fruit in us that looks like Him. His fruit is love, joy, peace, patience, kindness, goodness, faithfulness, gentleness, and self-control. Don't you want a spiritual tree that is dangling with all those fruits? I do!!

When we understand that it's not just the parable of the sower but also the parable of the soil, it changes everything!

Over the next several chapters, we will study and learn about the aspects of our lives that steal and stunt our growth in Him. The first passage we will read is about a farmer who went out to sow His seed. Jesus makes it very clear in His Word that God is the farmer. He is the Master Gardener. His Word is the seed. Our hearts are the soil. He is the one who is always and continually scattering His seed over us. The enemy's number one pursuit is to attempt to steal, kill, and destroy God's word from our hearts.

> A farmer went out to sow his seed. As he was scattering
> the seed, some fell along the path, and the birds came
> and snatched it up.
> Matthew 13:3-4

Seeds were scattered.

They fell upon the path.

The farmer was faithful.

The scripture says that the birds of the air came along and snatched the seeds up. The birds of the air represent the work of the enemy. They steal good seeds that are falling over our hearts before they ever get the opportunity to germinate.

I call these "bird snatchers" the distractions in our lives, and if you let them, they will snatch up every good thing pouring down over you. They will snatch up any attempt at finding healing and meaning. These distractions will interrupt your purpose in finding new life and new growth. They will snatch up dreams. They will snatch up callings. Distractions are a huge tool of Satan's. Although distractions don't immediately lead to eternal death, they can certainly kill our dreams, damage our relationships, and rob us of all that God has for us.

To me, one of the most intriguing Bible stories is found in Genesis 25-27. If you haven't read the entire story of Jacob and Esau, you need to! Esau was the eldest twin, and the custom during those times was for the eldest male to be the receiver of their father's double portion of the family inheritance. This double portion conveyed that the eldest male preserved the family lineage. They were the ones who held a position of honor, respect, authority, and financial security.

Jacob, the younger twin, barters his brother Esau out of his birthright and blessing for nothing more than a bowl of red stew. Out of desperation and an achy stomach, Esau forsakes what is rightfully his and gives his inheritance to Jacob. It seems ridiculous! How does this even happen? How does an entire inheritance get traded for something as small as a bowl of beans?

There are so many stories in Scripture where biblical characters act and respond in ways that baffle me! It is very tempting to look at them and wonder how they even got in the predicaments that they did. However, when I take time to reflect on my own life, I am less tempted to judge.

I would like to think that I am not capable of trading something of such precious value for something temporary and finite, but the truth is that it can happen all the time. It has in my own life over the years. We have this precious inheritance of an abundant earthly life and an eternal life to be found and experienced through Jesus. In theory, every decision we make should align with the path that will lead us to abundant living. Yet, in my story, there are moments where, in my aches, I trade my inheritance for the equivalence of just a bowl of beans.

I grew up knowing that preserving my purity for the man that God had for me was of high value and worth. And yet, in one of the most desperate seasons of my life, I traded my virginity for what I thought would take away the pain, the lack, the hunger and ultimately offer me love, acceptance, and security.

As I've matured and found Jesus, I still find myself trading all that He has for me for things that continue to seem as absurd as bowls of beans. I know that engaging and participating in conversations woven with juicy gossip are not valuable, nor are they pleasing to Him. And yet, I trade abundant living in Him for the temporary comfort of not always redirecting and blatantly ending those conversations.

I know that having the daily discipline to lead my children in His Word brings forth an abundant spiritual investment. And yet, I find myself letting so many other temporary, worldly things creep into our evening routines. I find myself robotically staggering to bed without ever making it a priority. I've traded an inheritance for a bowl of beans.

I know that living in the moment with my kids will reap rewards that this earth couldn't touch. And yet, I find my face cast downwards to whatever is happening on the screen of my phone. I trade the inheritance of that moment and what it has the opportunity to birth and produce for a bowl of beans.

I know that offering my body the proper nourishment, rest and exercise it needs to be abundantly fueled is honoring Him who gave it to me. And yet, I find myself pigging out, staying up way too late, and resisting opportunities to take care of it. I'm trading it for a bowl of beans–or in this case, Doritos and a slice of greasy pizza.

I know that serving my husband in ways that fill his cup heaps abundance, blessing and joy over our marriage. Even so, I find myself pouring into everything and everyone but him and then collapsing after a long day instead. I've traded it for a bowl of beans.

I know that social media is not a full representation of our lives–it's just the highlight reels. And yet, I find myself feeling tempted to document all the accolades, too. At the end of the day, it's all for just a bowl of beans.

It's all just Instant Beans.

Esau and Jacob were both hungry. Esau was hungry for food that was temporary. Jacob was hungry for an inheritance that would last forever. Has instant anything ever been better than the real thing? Our culture today shortcuts everything. The process is often lost in the pursuit of speed and instant gratification. We have become conditioned to seek out the quick and easy over the purposeful and deliberate. The idea of waiting for anything seems foreign and absurd.

As I was out watering one morning, I found the most beautiful Dahlia hidden underneath a pile of leafy greens in an old metal container. I got a glimpse of it as I bent down low. I had to push aside those big leafy greens that were attempting to cover up this delightful surprise!

God spoke over me in such a treasured way:

"Sweet child, the loudest things aren't always the things that need to be heard."

The leaves are the loud things. They represent all the distractions that are laying cover over the hidden blessings that God has for us.

There *is* the goodness of God over your life. It's there.

there are so many
good seeds that are
being planted in the
soil of our lives,
but we've left the
soil unattended.

He, as the farmer, is faithful to scatter good seeds over the soil of your life. Pay attention to what distractions are covering up that goodness. Stay in a posture of readiness. Stay in a posture of anticipated discovery of the beauty of God in your life.

It doesn't take a long time for us to create habits in our lives. Studies show that it only takes 30 days of doing the same thing for it to become a habit in your life. Early on in my spiritual growth journey, I began noticing how easy it was for me to miss all of the good things that God was pouring down over my life. Living mindlessly and unintentionally results in a life of missed moments and opportunities. We begin to create this habit of trampling over all the good things and miss uncovering all the blessings.

It's so easy to become lazy with our days and monotonously just exist. It's so easy to let the loudest things become the things we allow to lead us. It's too easy to miss unexpected surprises because they are crowded out by things that really don't matter. It's mindlessly and effortlessly easy. It's happening everywhere…all around us.

Dinner is served, and instead, your thumb is scrolling the lives of people you barely know while your family eats in your absence. Now, something you are supposed to talk about with your child or spouse gets snatched away. A life you were supposed to invest in gets snatched because you were distracted. You let the bird take it! It's this dangerous place of mindlessness.

How many times has something been snatched from your life, in seed form, before it ever had a chance to reap a harvest? Most of the time, we are distracted by things that hold very little eternal reward.

I was thinking the other day about how often technology is the source of so many of my distractions. Technology makes our lives insignificantly efficient. For instance, we no longer take pictures to pass down our family legacies. We take pictures to post on social media to see how many likes we can get. We post to grow our accounts and to feel validated, seen, applauded, and recognized.

How many of us have taken a picture like 14 times to try and produce this perfect image to post on Instagram? How often have we seen our kids doing something really cute, and we ask them to hold the pose, but by the end of accomplishing our documented shot for the social media world, we have trampled over the pureness of the moment? We live in a world now where the moment we take a picture, we are manufacturing the moment rather than maximizing a moment. Everything is so loud. But what if it didn't have to be? What if we didn't allow it to be?

We need to skim off the distractions.

We need to drown out the loud and choose to intentionally listen for the still, the small.

We desperately need to bend down low and uncover the hidden things around us.

We need to encounter the blessing that could be right beneath us.

Just as God spoke to me that morning, maybe the real beauty to be found is something more delicate, more tender, more still...more treasured!

There is so much good stuff coming down over our lives. There are so many good seeds that are being planted in the soil of our lives, but we've left the soil unattended, unprotected, and vulnerable to the work of the enemy. We have to refuse to allow things that are eternally important in our lives get snatched by things that seem urgent–that don't matter!!

The Lord has given us important tasks and assignments to accomplish and partake with Him each day. Distractions are lethal. They are the birds of the air that are hovering over the soil of our field ready and waiting to steal these tasks and assignments that God has for you. When we live unaware of these birds of the air, we bounce frantically from one obligation to the next, from one message to the next, from one phone to the next, from one social media site to the next. Everything seems so urgent and so important. It's all just noise.

What we really need is for the soil of our hearts to be in a state of readiness for every sprout of seed that He has assigned for us. There are so many seeds–so many good things being scattered on the soil of our fields, and if we aren't careful, we will let the birds take it! It is imperative that we stay in a state of readiness each and every day in order to grow during seasons of deep distractions. There are many ways to remain in a state of readiness. A few applicable ways that I stay in a state of readiness are:

- Staying in His Word daily (2 Timothy 3:16-17, Psalm 119:105)
- Listening for His voice (John 10:27)
- Taking every thought captive to the obedience of Christ (2 Corinthians 10:5)
- Speaking the promises of God over my life (Psalm 145:13)

- Identifying and reflecting on my priorities (Matthew 6:33, Luke 12:34)
- Leveraging my personal values in order to set clear goals (Proverbs 3:5-6, Proverbs 16:3, Philippians 3:13-14)
- Practicing daily gratitude (1 Thessalonians 5:16-18, Psalm 9:1-2)
- Living intentionally in the moment and in anticipation of seeds that He is scattering (Ephesians 2:10, Ephesians 5:10).

These are just a few of the ways that you can stay in a state of readiness in order to have the ability and awareness to identify the "bird snatchers" in your soil.

A good gardener knows to add certain material to the soil to increase its fruitfulness. In the same way, we must inject the practice of studying, reading & meditating on God's word. This adds richness to our hearts and gives us the spiritual nutrition we need. We must partner with God in working the soil of our hearts.

I find that the more I open my heart and mind to understand God's word, the more I rely on it for everything. It truly has become the nourishment to my soil. Its substance is unmatched. No substitution fills me as His word does. It's daily manna. I need it.

A good gardener knows that seeds need protection.

A good gardener knows that they may need to take a spade to hardened areas of their soul.

A good gardener knows that great discipline is required in order to pull out weeds of sin in their lives.

A good gardener trusts that all this is necessary in order to yield a field that flourishes.

Every soil has potential. Every field can be tilled and prepared to become a better place for the seed of God's word to grow & yield fruit. A surrendered field that is prepared, willing, available, faithful, and ready gives God the workspace to unfold the flourishing plans that He has for us. It is in this prepared place that He not only sows the seed of His Word but also produces a yield beyond our wildest expectations—a yield of 30, 60, or 100 times what was sown.

Our job is to prepare the soil. God's job is to sow and bring the increase. All the nourishment we need is right at our fingertips in God's Word.

REFLECT

- What are some ways that the enemy is using to snatch away God's truth from your heart?
- What distractions might be keeping you from experiencing the fruit of the good seed that is falling over you today?
- What changes and sacrifices are you choosing to make in order to prepare your heart for God's word—so it can mature and produce fruit?
- What is your response when you consider all that God can multiply through you and your obedience?

SCRIPTURE

> I ask God to make you intelligent and discerning in knowing Him personally—that the eyes of your heart would be focused and clear so that you can see exactly what it is that He is calling you to do & grasp the immensity of this glorious way of life that He has for you.
> Ephesians 1:16-18

PRAYER

God, I am asking You to help me fix my focus today and in this season where You have planted and placed me. I desire to grow in a deeper relationship with You and others in meaningful ways. I know You are scattering good seeds and raining down your blessing over the soil of my life. I don't want to miss all that You have for me. I know You have called me to do great things for You—that can't be accomplished while I am unfocused. Be it people, places or things, let nothing and no one interrupt the calling you have placed on my life. Help me to listen to Your still, small voice. In Jesus' name. Amen.

CHAPTER EIGHT
Seeds That Get Scorched

A farmer went out to sow his seed. As he was scattering the seed, some fell on rocky places, where it did not have much soil. It sprang up quickly, because the soil was shallow. But when the sun came up, the plants were scorched, and they withered because they had no root.
Matthew 13:5-6

"Full of rocks." Many farmers and gardeners know that rocks keep roots from delving deep into the ground. The results are that plants never receive the nutrients they need to help them become strong and yield fruit.

Did you know seeds germinate quickly in a rocky field because the soil is shallow?

Seeds can grow in rocky places and sprout something up really quickly because of the lack of good, rich soil. We can be surrounded by the wrong things and deceived by quick growth shoots.

Rocks represent hardship and persecution. You know the saying, "in the middle of a rock and a hard place." Some days in our spiritual growth journey, it can feel like that–hard pressed on every side. When we are in hardship and persecution, it can prevent roots from growing deep. People with rocks in their soil receive the Word of God at first, believing for a little while but falling away from Him in times of testing. We can't even bear fruit because of the rocks.

The one with a field full of rocks is rarely full of love, joy, peace, self-control, patience, kindness, goodness, faithfulness, and gentleness.

We have the ability to sprout things above the surface pretty quickly, but they are shallow. They may have the initial dazzle of something really impressive, but at the core, it's just another thing that didn't last.

We can say we trust God when our bank accounts are full. We can worship Him with hands raised when our spouse and kids are healthy. We can attest to His goodness when everything falls into place: when we love our job, when our kids follow the Lord, when we live inside the luxuries of all that we need, and more.

But do we trust Him when we can't make ends meet and truly need Him to be our provision?

Can we still lift our hands in worship when we receive a diagnosis that is terminal or when we are experiencing excruciating loss?

Can we still speak of His goodness when it feels like everything is falling apart: when we lose our job, when our kids aren't following Him, when we can't even scrape by?

We can say we love Jesus, attend church every Sunday, post a verse here and there on social media, wear our cross necklace, and yet wither with no root because it's all shallow.

We know that rocks in our soil can be detrimental to our growth. They hinder us from growing deep roots. We need deep roots in order to withstand savage storms that will come into our lives and attack our fields. As I have mentored different women over the years, I have told many of them multiple times this truth: If only I knew back then what I know right now.

Nothing was wasted in His hands.

There have been seasons of God's planting that felt really hard. With it came shovels full of undesirable soil. There was a lot of hardship and persecution. The ground felt unwelcoming and cold. And yet, had I had the mind of Christ when those pebbles were placed amongst my field, I would've responded to that hardship drastically differently than I did back then.

There will continually be pebbles, rocks, maybe even boulders that find their way into your field. What if we had the mind of Christ? What if we set our minds on things above? If we have the mind of Christ, our responses to these hardships could be the very fertilizing agent that offers the development in us for the right elements to a strong root system. What if we considered it only joy every time we faced hardship and persecution? His Word in James 1:2-4 says this:

> Count it all joy, my brothers, when you meet trials of various kinds, for you know that the testing of your faith produces steadfastness. Let steadfastness have its full effect, that you may be perfect and complete, lacking in nothing.

Now, THAT would be a root system that could withstand the raging, savage storms in your life!

In the parable of the seeds that get scorched found in Matthew, Jesus goes on further and shares how the heat of the sun is what scorches the first bits of growth.

> But when the sun came up, the plants were scorched.

Sometimes, the physical condition of my heart can easily be described as sun-scorched. There are just days where spiritually, it feels like drought. There are days I feel like that tiny, little tomato plant that has barely sprouted and is already shriveling under the blazing sun. The heat index of my life's circumstances can make it hard even to breathe some days.

It may feel like the torches of trials are scorching you. The heat may be beating down upon you in this season as you navigate some really hard obstacles.

You may be in the very center of a scary diagnosis, and it feels like hope is a long way off.

You may be battling trauma that sweeps you under the current of the most fierce and abusive waves you have ever encountered. You wonder if the hurt will ever let up enough for you to catch your breath.

You may have fists in the air with rage, not knowing that it is grief that you are trying to navigate. The heaviness you feel isn't something you feel equipped to process on your own.

You may feel like you are crushed under the weight of all of life's demands and can't even begin to fathom how ends will meet or how days will feel fulfilling again.

You may be struggling to find peace and unity with someone in your life, where it feels like no amount of proving yourself true will ever be enough.

You may have a wandering child, which leads to a smoldering of doubts where the enemy attempts to pin down every "what-if" through your shortcomings over the years.

You may be experiencing the unfaithfulness or detachment of your partner or close friend and find yourself struggling even to feel desirable, noticed, and loved.

You may be asked to stay in a place that feels unsafe and unwelcoming, a place where you are continually getting hurt by someone.

The heat from the trials of our lives can feel unbearably hot. The heat from the trials can breed anger and frustration if we are not careful. The heat can stunt our growth.

One of my favorite Bible verses talks about God's promise in our lives during hot seasons.

> The Lord will guide you always; He will satisfy your needs in a sun-scorched land and will strengthen your frame.
> Isaiah 58:11

His word in Matthew 13 doesn't say that the plant died because of the heat. The plant was only scorched because of the heat. The plant died because it had no roots. That's a huge difference. It's the lack of a deep root system that killed the plant. Not the heat.

We can walk through fiery furnaces and live.

We can walk through unimaginable resistance and trauma and live.

We can be placed in environments that we thought would kill us and live.

We can be hard-pressed on every side but not crushed, perplexed but not abandoned, struck down but not destroyed.

His Word in 2 Corinthians 4 tells us that.

We may be scorched, but sometimes it's the scorching that is part of the story. It's not what defines us. But it is part of the story. It's part of us. It's not the heat that killed the plant, and it's not the heat that will kill us spiritually. Having no root system will.

We need a deeper root system, friends.

Growing roots is the most important part of the Christian journey.

The primary purpose of a plant's root system is to absorb all the water and food to keep the plant growing so it can withstand storms and support the plant.

Jesus is the living water for us. When we believe in Him, we are promised to receive His living water that will never run out. We have sustenance of life through Him. It is a living well of water that will forever feed us, nourish us, and help us to grow and flourish in every circumstance and throughout every season of our lives.

> They withered because they had no root.
> Matthew 13:6

As you are in seasons of growing in this spiritual journey and the heat of life sweats over you, I pray you make worship a priority in the midst of it.

Worship, I have found, is one of the most imperative nutrients that waters and cultivates. It keeps my soul and my roots growing in the sun-scorched spaces.

It doesn't replace the living water. Worship is the method to receive the living water! It's the transferring agent.

It is not unusual for there to be worship music playing throughout our house at all times during the day, especially during our morning routine. One morning, as music played in the background, I came into the dining room to catch a glimpse.

Worship in its purest posture. Untainted. Untamed.

These lyrics played in the backdrop of my daughter's offering and worship:

🎵 It may look like I'm surrounded but I'm surrounded by You... this is how I fight my battles 🎵

And I couldn't take my gaze off of her. I just kept thinking...She doesn't really fully know yet. She has no clue the lengths and depths that the enemy will go to attempt to devour her in the heat of the day.

But she will soon find out.

Even greater so, she has no clue about the lengths and depths that God will go to refresh her.

But she will soon find out.

I needed the reminder that day. Even now, as you are reading this, you may need it, too.

Lift your hands and declare this promise over your life today.

Lift your hands in battle.

Lift your hands in worship.

Lift your hands in the smallest substance of faith that you can muster.

Lift your hands in surrender.

Because THIS is how we fight our battles!

When we go through fierce seasons, it can feel difficult to bring Him our worship. It is easy to rebel against this type of offering in seasons of heartache and disappointment. The enemy can corrupt, taint, and disrupt our hearts and minds to the point of depletion–where worshipping God becomes nearly non-existent in these trying times. It's hard to sing a song of praise when the heat is scorching us. Friends, when we refuse to worship because of the heat that we are under, we can be promised that it will kill our spiritual life.

Psalm 23 held me during this season of my Babylon. His word in verses 5-6 says:

> You prepare a table before me in the presence of my enemies. You anoint my head with oil; my cup overflows. Surely Your goodness and mercy will follow me all the days of my life, and I will dwell in the house of the Lord forever.

Did y'all catch that? It's not us that prepares the table in the presence of our enemies. It's Him. He prepares the table for us in the presence of our enemies. That word "prepare" is "ta-a-rok" in Hebrew. It literally means "to arrange." God is arranging every detail of our lives so that we can feast on all that He has for us.

When we can worship Him in the midst of whatever the enemy is surrounding us in, the care of the Host of Hosts, God Himself, will give us a kind of treatment that will blow our minds! We can sit and rest at the banquet table under His care and protection while the enemy looks on.

Let me be very clear here. If your enemy has skin, you have the wrong enemy.

In our flesh and humanness, it's easy to make people in our lives our enemy. His word does not validate that stance. His Word in Ephesians 6:12 says that our struggle is not against flesh and blood but against the powers of this dark world and against the spiritual forces of evil in the heavenly realms.

The context of the table prepared for us in the presence of our enemies, in Psalm 23, is from the last supper before Jesus was betrayed and crucified.

Do you know who also was at the table with Jesus that night?

His betrayer, Judas.

Do you know why?

Judas had a seat at the table that night because Jesus arranged for him to have one.

Jesus was surrounded by people who said they loved him and still betrayed Him. Jesus knew all that and still arranged a seat at the table for them.

Notice that the care of the Host, God, doesn't eliminate the presence of our enemies. It enables the experience of God's goodness and bounty even in their midst. He has the bounty to feed us and the power to protect us. It's His bounty of living water that gives us the sustenance to undergo the heat with a deep root system.

Jesus was able to arrange a seat at the table in the midst of His greatest betrayer and serve Judas the night before His death because He was a worshipper with deep roots. He stayed attached to God. He was saturated in prayer and praise. In the hottest moment of Jesus' life, what did God do? He prepared and arranged a table in the presence of His enemy. In the hottest moment of Jesus' life, He bore more fruit than we can even imagine.

Why do we think that heat seasons mean that God has forgotten about us? The hottest moments of our lives could be the very ones where He is arranging a table for us to feast. The hottest seasons of our lives could be the very ones where He is nourishing us like never before.

Heat seasons are not evidence that God has forgotten about us. Heat seasons are evidence that He's feeding us so we can bear more fruit than ever.

We allow so much to disrupt and inhibit our worship. Had Jesus opposed worship and walked in disobedience that night, it may not have led to His crucifixion. His crucifixion is what offers us freedom. His obedience is ultimately what allows us to have the assurance of eternal life.

In the pruning segment, we will talk about what it looks like to die to self. For now, we should ponder the gift of crucifixion. If our deepest pains lead to the greatest bounty, shouldn't we stop opposing it and learn to worship in it?

We can sit down at a prepared table and eat in perfect peace.

We can grow in what feels like undesirable soil because we have living water.

When we can trust Him in this way, that is worship.

That is when you begin developing deep roots. I know that when the posture of my heart is that of gratitude, thankfulness, and praise, I am growing deep roots. I literally could feel these roots spiritually taking off. When we choose not to be victims, but warriors, we are growing deep roots. When we can set aside self-righteousness for His example of righteousness, we grow deep roots. It is a process. It doesn't happen overnight. It is a process of surrendering to the Lord over and over again.

I learned how to worship outside of my circumstances and then how to worship inside of them. That takes deeper roots and deeper growth. To worship in the undesirable soil, in what seemed like "winter season," harsh and cold, and in a foreign field. I learned that my worship was my weapon. It's the antidote for the heat. With hands held high and knees bent low.

When you can worship when you don't feel it, when you can praise His name when you are standing on the edge of everything scary, when you can trust Him when the odds are stacked against you, when you can raise your hands and declare that you are surrendering in the heat of it all, when you can arrange a seat in your midst for someone who has wronged you, when you can wash the feet of your betrayer, you have sliced the enemy in two.

Try to worship and hold a grudge.

Try to worship and stay mad at your spouse.

Try to worship and maintain complete hatred and bitterness.

Worship is our weapon.

It's what puts everything else in its place—including Satan himself.

It defeats the devil's foothold that he uses in our hearts and minds to steal joy, kill our destiny, and destroy Holy Spirit movements in our lives.

It's about Jesus. He is worthy of our praise! He is worthy of our offering to Him—even in the heat.

Worship can't be rooted in anything other than who He is; otherwise, it won't be deep enough.

We are called to let our roots grow down in Him. And yet, so often, we want to flourish in the "above ground" spaces that are visible to those around us, but God wants our deep. God wants us to grow DOWN in Him so that our lives are built upon Him—and nothing else.

The above-ground growth may seem impressive, but it doesn't move the heart of God. He knows that the above ground will come, and your lives will be a blessing to those around you, but it must first be anchored in what's happening in the deep.

When our fields are full of rocks, we become people who respond with initial enthusiasm, but the word of God does not sink in deep. When persecution or hard times come along, we are tempted to give up at once. We can't withstand the scorch of the trials and tribulations if our root systems are shallow. We won't be able to weather the storms without depth. We won't be able to experience His lasting joy if we focus on what's happening around us.

Happiness depends on happenings.

Joy depends on Christ.

How many times have you found yourself living life at a superficial and shallow level?

You may have returned all of your messages today and yet didn't impact eternity in any intentional way.

You checked everything off your list but didn't even have time to meet with Him.

You spent hours mindlessly scrolling through your phone and yet don't even know who your kids are hanging out with!

Do you know why this is so dangerous? It's dangerous because it has this appearance of life, but it's not really life! The seeds are planted, but no root has grown. It has given the appearance of productivity, but it's not productive.

Roots represent commitment.

They represent what you're tethered to.

The problem isn't that we are unrooted. The problem is that we are wrongly rooted. So many of us are tethered to the wrong things. No wonder we are so easily distracted, disappointed, and full of doubt.

Roots represent commitment. They represent what we are tethered to. The problem isn't that we are unrooted. The problem is that we are wrongly rooted.

REFLECT

- Part of preparing the soil of our hearts to receive from the Lord is removing the rocks (the hard things) in our field. Removing the rocks gives us the ability to establish deep roots. What "rocks" can you identify in your field?
- How do "rocks" in our hearts prevent God's roots from moving deeper into our souls?
- What tools might you use to remove these rocks?
- Allowing our lives to be built upon Him means that spiritually we have to have deep roots. How can you take small steps today to develop deeper roots through His Word?
- How can you worship Him in the heat of this season?

SCRIPTURE

> Let your roots grow DOWN in Him & let your
> lives be built on Him. Then your faith will grow strong
> in the truth you were taught, and you will overflow
> with thankfulness.
> Colossians 2:7

PRAYER

I pray that out of His glorious riches He may strengthen you with power through His Spirit in your inner being, so that Christ may dwell in your hearts through faith. I pray that you, being rooted and established in love, may have power, together with all the Lord's holy people, to grasp how wide and long and high and deep is the love of Christ, and to know this love that surpasses knowledge—that you may be filled to the measure of all the fullness of God. Ephesians 3:16-19

CHAPTER NINE
Seeds That Get Choked

> Other seed fell among thorns, which grew up and choked the plants. He hears the Word, and the cares of this world and the deceitfulness of riches choke the word, and he becomes unfruitful.
> Matthew 13:7 & 13:22-23

There are seasons of our lives where the word of God takes root and begins to grow. Yet, in the midst of the growth, there are thorns.

How did these thorns get in the soil?

Thorns grow in the soil of our fields when we have exposed our hearts to a lot of different seeds that aren't from God. I call these, "foreign seeds". We have to steward what we listen to and what we spend our time and affection on.

The thorns can represent a multitude of things: bitterness, envy, jealousy, lack of thankfulness, discontentment, rebellion, anger, worry, anxiety, and desire for worldly things. When thorns begin to grow up next to the good things that God has planted over the soil of our lives, they can exhaust those good things and ultimately choke them out. It is an attempt at strangulation of God's goodness over our lives. There's now competition for our time, attention, and affection. These thorns in our lives become a threat to the health and maturation of our lives. This is where a lot of people live. We start to activate the Word of God in our lives, but it gets suffocated. Any flourishing fruit that was available is now shriveled and malnourished.

As you are maturing in Christ, is there still this tug to pursue things of this world to fulfill you? We are called to bear fruit for Him.

So, what makes our lives unfruitful?

A major source of our lack of fruitfulness can be directly linked to the things of the mind: what we think about, where we spend our time, what we spend our money on, and what rules our thoughts. Whoever and whatever governs our attention governs our actions.

The worries of this life are making it unfruitful.

Notice the line didn't say "the responsibilities." It's not what we are asked to do that chokes us. It's us worrying that does. We are distracted by the interpretation of what we believe is going on in our lives. If I were the devil, I'd play this card all day long. He can destroy us by distracting us without even doing anything to us, just making us believe it COULD happen. Just worrying about what could happen can suffocate us and choke us! The enemy is crafty that way.

By the power of automatic suggestion, we choke ourselves through a distracted mind.

Ever since I was a kid, I can remember being worried about money– not wanting more of it but being worried about not having enough. There were seasons growing up where money was a little tight. My parents had four kids. That says enough. But we always had everything we needed.

My mom would always joke as I got older that anytime she ever bought me anything, I would always respond by asking, "How much was it?"

There was always this worry inside of me of a lack of provision, and that continued into adulthood and early married life. Even my husband will admit to you that he had to correct me from time to time.

When a bill would come in the mail, I didn't even want to open it. I would clam up.

When he would want to go out to dinner at a nice, expensive restaurant for our anniversary, I would try and suggest something more affordable.

When he would try to surprise me by bringing home flowers or high-end chocolate-dipped strawberries for an anniversary, I would tense up at the thought of how much he had to have spent.

My husband is a frugal man who is responsible with his spending and faithful in his stewardship of his paycheck, but even so, I lived in a constant state of worry. It hindered my initial years in my spiritual walk. Whenever the Lord would ask me to bless someone monetarily, I would be resistant, thinking about all of the financial obligations we had to take care of for ourselves.

Whenever I first became convicted of not tithing and giving my 10% back to God through my paychecks, as He asks of us, I became angry and frustrated with the conviction. "We can barely make ends meet as it is. How in the world are we going to be able to take care of everything once I give up 10%?" My worry choked me.

I lived in this constant state of distrust in the Lord to meet every need and bring every provision. It started small, but it bred and gave birth to so much more. It used to be money that I worried about, and then it became my marriage, and then my kids, and then my relationships at work and church, and then my calling, and then my relationship with God. It never ended.

This worrying nature, which truly was a lack of trust in God's ability and provisions, corrupted every assignment that the Lord had for me. It became this excessive cultivation over the field of my heart. Worry acted as a tiller. Initially, it seemed harmless, but the overworking and the intense cultivation left the soil of my heart and mind exposed, exhausted, depleted, and vulnerable to being washed away. My mind was being choked through worry and anxiety and fear. Those three things began to feed every thought I had and lead every decision I made.

Several years ago, a neuroscience study was done that proved that gratitude and anxiety cannot exist in the brain at the same time. Let that sink in.

Being deceived by the enemy can strangle every good seed that God has for us if we aren't careful.

You may be walking through heartache or hardship that you feel like you just can't get over. Worry may have your mind held captive. Anxiety may be trying to take the front seat of your life and overwork the soil of your heart. When you don't know what to do, begin to worship. Do not let your worry be louder than your worship. Our God is not dependent upon feelings. He is who He is, regardless of what is going on.

Worship may not change your set of circumstances, but worship will change you.

So, where is your mind parked?

Every moment of every single day, we sow something into our lives–something that produces life or something that doesn't.

Change your mind, and it will change how you see what is going on, even if none of the circumstances change! You need to come up for air because you're being choked and distracted.

It's not people or circumstances that are distracting you, it's your mind that is distracting you! Scripture goes on to say,

> The deceitfulness of riches and
> wealth chokes out the Word.

The world tries to make us believe the lie that riches and wealth are the goal of life. There's this screaming philosophy spoken through every celebrity, every commercial, every social media platform, every new car/house that our neighbors are purchasing–it's all dangled in front of us like this carrot of success. If we aren't careful, we may find ourselves doing whatever it takes to get the next raise, the next best thing, by comparing ourselves to others. With that comes this tragic and dangerous question, "Have I made it?"

Another lie that the world tries to make us believe is that money is the key to security. We've all heard it: income strategies, wealth hacks, extreme frugality, etc. Financial independence is trending everywhere. There's nothing wrong with being financially independent. It can promise freedom and security, which is so alluring. The promise of never having to live paycheck to paycheck offers us an illusion of security.

The truth is this: there is no genuine security in riches.

You can lose it all in a moment. Money cannot and should not be trusted to protect us. Even Solomon said,

> He who trusts in his own riches will fall. But the
> righteous will flourish like the green leaf.

There's this deceiving nature about money that promises us pleasure and fulfillment if we gain a little bit more. But we are always left feeling more empty and more unfulfilled. It's the "Kool-aid." I think we've all been here. We may still battle in this area of our lives. God desires for our character to be free from the love of money and be content with what we have. God desires this because He knows that we cannot serve both God and money.

Over the span of most of my early life, I had never been tempted to conform drastically. Forfeiting any part of me in an attempt to fit in wasn't anything I had ever encountered before in any depth. It just wasn't an area of my life that really ever taunted me. However, that day did come.

I can vividly remember serving in an area of ministry and seeing all of the other women wearing this specific brand of dress that had just become really popular at that time. It became very apparent to me that I was the only one who didn't have one.

The enemy has a way of magnifying our lack.

That realization began to bother me. Envy and jealousy began deceiving me and corrupting God's plan and purpose over my life. I didn't have a lot of extra money at that time in my life. We were literally just making ends meet as an early married couple. But I cashed in my change jar and took the couple bags of pop cans that we had collected in the garage, and I went and purchased one of those dresses. Honestly, I didn't even like the look of the dress.

Dave Ramsey coined this phrase, "We buy things we don't need with money we don't have to impress people we don't like."

That seems pretty straightforward. I'll cut out the last part because that piece doesn't fully apply to my story. However, there's a whole lot of truth to that statement. I didn't have the money to buy a dress like that, and certainly not a dress that I didn't even like!

His Word says that the deceitfulness of riches and the desire for other things can choke us out. They can strangle every good thing He has for us if we aren't careful. It's not the riches that choke us out. It's being deceived by them. It took me many years to realize that the bitterness, envy, and jealousy that had become a stronghold in my life birthed into something much more dangerous. That stronghold led to a seeking of worldly things as a sense of belonging. I didn't even desire riches or possessions, but the enemy is tricky that way. He can entice you to desire something you don't even care about in an attempt to fill a void of something that is shattering in a different area of your life. Riches cannot deceive us unless we put our trust in them. I had begun putting my trust in something that I had no clue was the source of my spiritual strangulation.

I wonder how much of your life you spend reaching for the wrong things? I wonder how many times we've traded something eternal for something temporary?

Paul says it best in Philippians 3:7:

> Whatever was gained to me, I now consider loss. The very credentials these people are waving around as something special, I'm tearing up and throwing out with the trash—along with everything else I used to take credit for. And why? Because Christ. Yes, all the things I once thought were so important are gone from my life. Compared to the high privilege of knowing Jesus Christ as my Master, everything I once thought I had going for me is insignificant. I've dumped it all in the trash so that I could embrace Christ and be embraced by Him. I didn't want some petty, inferior brand of righteousness. I gave up all that inferior stuff so I could know Christ personally.
> Philippians 3:7-10 MSG

To summarize, he said, "I got the goals and then I realized the goals I was holding on to were the very things that were keeping me from what God was trying to give me. Whatever was gained to me, I now consider loss. I've got better goals and gains for the sake of Christ." Paul said, "I spent so much of my life reaching for the wrong things."

I believe that if we are honest with ourselves, we have been reaching for the wrong things, too. When our hands are stretched towards anything besides Jesus, it's the wrong thing.

We can be full of everything but Christ and still be empty.

God doesn't say that good ground has no rocks or no thorns. What He says is that good ground has no rocks or thorns that hinder its growth through fruitfulness. There may be rocks in your field. There may be thorns in your field. Identify them. Pluck them out. Don't allow them to hinder your growth. Protect your field–it's the place you're going to grow.

REFLECT

- What are things that consume your mind through worry, that are making you unable to be used fully for the Lord? Name those things/areas.
- We read that gratitude and anxiety cannot coexist in the brain at the same time. How does this encourage you?
- How can you create a habit to spend time in His Word and in a posture of worship daily? Write down when and where each day you will make this possible.
- What are the thorns in your life that are attempting to choke out God's word?
- What worldly things do you find yourself continuously reaching for?
- What practical ways will you reach forward towards all that God is calling you to?

SCRIPTURE

> There is nothing on earth that I desire besides You.
> My flesh and heart may fail, but God is the strength of
> my heart and my portion forever.
> Psalm 73:25-26

> Seek first the Kingdom of Heaven and His
> righteousness, and all these things will be added to you.
> Matthew 6:33

PRAYER

Heavenly Father, forgive me for the times that I have allowed the riches and pleasures of this world to choke out Your Word in my heart. Search the soil of my heart and mind and reveal any thorns that are hidden there. Help us to nurture the seeds that You are sowing into our soil. We want to tend our own soul gardens so that we can bear much fruit for You. In Jesus' name, amen.

CHAPTER TEN

Seeds That Get Sabotaged

The kingdom of heaven is like a man who sowed good seed in his field. But while everyone was sleeping, his enemy came and sowed weeds among the wheat, and went away.
Matthew 13:24-26

You have a great destiny! God put His seed in you.

You also have a great enemy. Your enemy likes to catch you sleeping and plant weeds in your life!! He has done this to me so many times throughout my spiritual journey.

The enemy cannot take away your destiny. He can only plant something next to it that will make it difficult for you to recognize it. The

reference to weeds in Matthew 13 is the word "Zizanion" in Greek. It means false or fake. Sometimes, these weeds that grow up next to the flourishing wheat in our fields look so similar to the wheat that it is really difficult for us to discern one from the other. We don't always recognize the weeds of sin. They pop up, and before we know it, they are choking the life out of things we want to flourish. These weeds can be stumbling blocks, traps, temptations, selfishness, greed, self-promotion, and pride. They can also be activities or people that take our time and pull us away from Him. These weeds can also come in the form of lies that we've believed about ourselves, shame from past mistakes, or painful wounds.

I have left the soil of my mind unprotected. I have gotten caught up in the busyness of life and what I thought were priorities that I didn't even notice when the enemy snuck in! He came when I was sleeping, and he sabotaged my field. Weeds began to grow among the wheat!

I am learning the gravity and urgency of recognizing sin in my life and immediately asking God to uproot it before it chokes out the entire field.

In Bible times, farmers had to burn their fields that were infected with weeds so they could start over. We can't neglect the soil of our hearts and let spiritual weeds put down roots any longer! There may be a burning away that is required to remove everything we are clinging to that isn't fruitful.

It may feel like an undoing. It's really a becoming.

There are times where we need to strip the soil of everything that no longer serves the will of God for our lives.

Circumstances are not our problem. People aren't even the problem. The problem lies WITHIN.

The enemy is an intruder! Many of you reading this today are battling the enemy, not because you invited him in, but because he is a thief. He broke in, and for whatever reason, he still resides in you. He is still sabotaging your field!

You wake up every day tormented by thoughts that he placed in your head. Thoughts of doubt, insecurity, hopelessness, defeat, and oppression are stifling. This list goes on and on.

Is it possible to be a believer in Christ, in this day and age and be so rooted in Christ that you have a holy confidence that is not borrowed from the opinions of others or the circumstances around you? I know so!

So much of our lives are spent trying so hard to measure up to some standard that we saw somewhere that was imposed on us from some societal norm. This Snapchat society is one where we feel the pressure to make our lives look interesting for 10 seconds so people will think more highly of us.

There's a different reality that Paul wants us to understand: The fullness of Christ has been given to you!

I often have women ask me to help God reveal to them their calling. It usually goes something like this: "What does God want me to do?"

But it's not about what you "do."

God does not validate like people validate. People validate based on what you can do for them. People will validate based on the value that your actions carry that will contribute directly to their lives. God does not validate based on performance. He validates based on relationship. He did not validate what Jesus did. He validated who He *was*.

In Matthew 3:17, God called down from Heaven and said:

> This is my Beloved Son, whom I love;
> with Him, I am well pleased.

Did you catch that? God spoke identity over Jesus first. He wanted Jesus to be reminded of who He was in God. Next, God tells Him how much He loves him. Lastly, He speaks of His pleasure towards Jesus based on what Jesus did. All three are important. However, a reminder and clarification of identity was the first thing God spoke over Jesus.

There could be a multitude of reasons why. I believe it is because God knows that if we know who we are in Him, we will want to please Him.

When we know who we are in Him, the overflow of all that we say and do is of Him.

When our identity is secure through Him, we don't need the approval or validation of anyone but Him.

We can be fully satisfied through Him.

And I'm learning…*I can love people more when I need them less.*

That's why Jesus could love the way that He did. He needed them less. He needed them less than He needed His relationship with His Heavenly Father. Every act of obedience and service was sourced from the Father with love.

When you need people less, you can love them more.

When you don't need to be validated by them because you've already been validated by Him, everything changes.

I spent years seeking the validation of many by saying yes to every ministry in hopes that it would offer inclusion and belonging. I spent years seeking man's approval by abusing healthy boundaries that God was desiring for the health of my field. I spent years conforming to circles and settings that I knew weren't what He wanted for me out of fear of having nothing better. And what that created was a hollow, selfish kind of love for people. We can't love people the way we are called to love them when we need them to fulfill us in ways that only Jesus should.

We confuse being rooted in Christ with being rooted in productivity, performance, busyness, or even our achievements. We think we are deeply rooted, but we are actually just deeply busy for God.

When you need people less, you can respond in genuine love like this: "I appreciate you thinking of me. However, I can't say yes this time."

When you need people less, you no longer feel the pressure to explain why your Yes' are Yes' and your No's are No's because each have been ordered by the One who knows what is required for your growth. When you need people less, you come to the realization that no person, no activity, nothing, and no amount of striving will ever bring you the sense of purpose, fulfillment, and belonging that Jesus does.

We need to give ourselves permission to:

- Rest without justification
- Decline good opportunities that aren't God's current calling
- Trust that limits are part of God's design
- Take a break from saying yes to every ask
- Being honest

If we truly need people less, we work fully unto the Lord.

Imagine if we gave the Lord our full capacity at parenting, loving our spouse, forgiving our enemies, serving in our workspaces, tending our home? Your calling is more about fulfilling everything that God has placed on your life based on an *awareness of the fullness of Christ that already resides inside of you!* This is the death blow to every wrong spirit that has been spoken over you. Some truths that I often remind myself:

- Rest is necessary

- Small acts towards greater growth count
- Not every need is my calling
- Being faithful in a few things honors God more than being spread thin
- True rootedness isn't about doing more for God
- True rootedness is about *being* more with God

The main ambition of a calling is not about something that I do but rather more about someone that He wants me to BE! What I do is not for Him but rather from Him. There is a vast difference between living for God and living for God.

True freedom in Christ comes the moment you realize that you have nothing to prove to anyone because, in the fullness of Christ, God fully approves of you.

We have been given the fullness of Christ.

This is why Jesus was concerned about addressing sin in our lives—not just because of the appearance of the ugliness of the weeds, but because they choke out who we're becoming!

The enemy sees our calling and knows he doesn't have the power to take away our calling! But he thinks, "If I can get them so distracted by things of this world that hold no eternal value, they will spend their entire lives gathering up and investing into things all the while losing their very soul."

The devil plants the weeds. He doesn't have to stay. Because now YOU are watering it! He plants only a seed and says, "They won't even see it because they are sleeping."

It's imperative that we wake up from our spiritual slumber and see who is watering our field. If our water source is anything other than the living water, it's getting wet the wrong way.

true rootedness isn't
about doing more
for God.
true rootedness is
about being more
with God.

If our thirst is temporarily satisfied by water from a polluted source, we won't grow and flourish even if the soil is wet.

In John 4, the woman at the well encountered Jesus in a place she never thought He'd be, in her brokenness. The garden of her soul was full of rocks, roots that were shallower than all she was seeking, and soil that was wet from every polluted source. Yet, she was still thirsty. You will never fill your emptiness from a place of emptiness.

Jesus entered into the soil of her heart and said,

> Everyone who drinks this water will be thirsty again, but whoever drinks the water I give them will never thirst. Indeed, the water I give them will become in them a spring of water welling up to eternal life.

We have to wake up to what's happening around us. We have to pay careful attention to who is holding the watering can in our lives. The enemy wants us to become so busy and distracted that we don't even realize that he sows seeds among the wheat.

We can get caught up in the busyness of life, all the while feeling completely barren of any and all fulfillment. We can get choked out by the worries of this world. We can be caught spiritually sleeping, and the enemy comes in and begins to wreck our field. We need to uproot some sin and declare spiritual bankruptcy.

As weeds in our lives grow larger and larger, they become harder and harder to remove. Taking a careful look at your field may require you to identify sprouting weeds. The gardener who is willing to take a careful look at their field daily and weed is the one who will get to experience a flourishing field.

REFLECT

- What are ways that you are mindlessly lulled to sleep as the enemy breaks into your field?
- List some of the weeds that spring up regularly into the soil of your field.

Ask God to show you the next step to weeding your field.

SCRIPTURE

> A man shall not be established by wickedness: but
> the root of the righteous shall not be moved.
> Proverbs 12:3

PRAYER

Heavenly Father, we want to grow in intimacy with you. Draw us to you in humility, worship, and surrender. Put your hand on our lives and touch those weeds that hinder growth, either outright sin or just hindrances. Instruct us how to weed them out. We confess and repent and ask for help. We thank You for your constant faithfulness, forgiveness and presence in our lives. Give us a newfound desire to tend to our spiritual garden and weed our hearts. In Jesus' name, amen.

CHAPTER ELEVEN
100-Fold

The seed falling on good soil refers to someone who hears the word and understands it. This is the one who produces a crop, yielding a hundred, sixty, or thirty times what was sown.
Mark 4:20

Why does the sower, God, toss precious seeds into barren soil? If you ask any Farmer or Gardener, they will tell you that seed is precious. There is a strategy in where seeds are placed. Seeds can't just grow anywhere. However, this parable speaks of God tossing precious seed into soil where birds are snatching it up, into rocky soil where it withers, among the thorns where it eventually is strangled.

What would you think if you saw a farmer throwing seeds onto the road, onto a pile of rocks, into tangled thorns? This is where God chooses to throw His precious seed. This parable in the Bible is a story about a Sower who sows in strange places. I believe that this reveals a lot about God's character. He does not only send His Word to those who will receive it. God chooses to share His Word with even those who may reject it. The light of God's Word will always expose the darkness within each of us. His desire is that none of us perish but have abundant and everlasting life through Him. This is the character of God; He sends Himself out everywhere and to everyone. The Sower does not begin with the fertile field. He plants seeds first where there is little likelihood that they will grow. Even after this, He chooses to plant where seeds may even die. The field that is fertile isn't His first tossing, it's His fourth. His resources aren't limited.

I'd love to say that I'm always the good soil. That's just not the truth. I can have all kinds of soil in me from time to time. That's the truth. I can be the soil that allows the enemy to snatch God's Word from me when the kaleidoscope of other voices drowns out His Word. I can be the soil that initially receives what God says with joy, but then I fall away when I come up against something really hard. I can be the soil that allows worry to choke out my faith before it ever begins to bloom.

There are times when I reach out to God to get an answer instead of listening to hear from Him in awe and wonder. There are times when the distractions in my life disrupt any desire to meet with Him at all. There are times when rocks in my field make me feel hard-pressed on every side. That type of weight and pressure has made me resist Him. There are times when I am wrongly rooted and don't even know that it is Him I need. There are times when I am so suffocated by the thorns of life that I can't even breathe in once more to allow Him to fill my lungs. There are times when I have been spiritually asleep, and the enemy tiptoed in and began sowing all the wrong seeds in my field. In these moments, I can't even differentiate what voice is His. I would venture to guess that many of us have been in every type of soil throughout our lives.

Friends, we need to talk about this. How do we teach Sunday School for years, but when the opposition comes, we have no idea what to do with it?

How do we sit in service after service, but our seeds aren't even rooted? Instead, we are blown away at the slightest breath from the enemy.

How have we tricked ourselves into believing we are good soil when our field has little to no fruit from the harvest?

How can we pray elaborate prayers but find ourselves ineffective in applying the belief?

How can we carry around spiritual weapons to slaughter the enemy but have no clue how to use them?

This is the stuff.

We can know all the right things to say on Sunday mornings, but if we don't actually know how to apply them to the soil of our fields, it doesn't bring about a flourishing harvest.

I am more worldly minded when I'm not in His Word, not listening to worship music, and not spending time in prayer for others. When I focus on myself, I fall prey to the wrong soil. It is in these times when I can't receive Him. His gentle nudges to love others are snatched when I'm focused on my own hurt. His prompts to pray for my enemy are crowded out when all I can think about is the injustice. His gentle guidance will never get past my garden gates if I am not pursuing His heart.

The unfruitfulness of every soil type was not because the Word wasn't heard or because seeds weren't being sown. When Jesus described the soils, He mentioned specifically that every one of them heard God's word. The problem was not with *what* they heard. The problem was with *how* they heard. This is our problem. We hear the Word of God when we are already "full." Our impatient, spiritual stomachs have binged on junk food, and when the meat of His Word is set in front of us, we slide it aside because our appetite is gone. Every nourishment we desperately need in our soil has already been replaced by a counterfeit that makes us feed on the wrong thing.

Good, fertile soil does not appear all by itself. The Gardener changes the soil. Good soil left to itself will become weedy soil. Every field needs to be weeded. If the soil is shallow and full of rocks, the rocks can be broken up and removed. Farmers and gardeners have been improving their plots of land even before the time of Jesus. The Gardener we have through God is the one who does miracles. We have a Gardener who will work the soil in an attempt to make it good soil that produces a flourishing crop. The word "good" is "kailos" in Greek. It means "honorable moment or season" for harvest time.

I want to be a receiver of His Word.

I want it to grow and produce all the good God desires in my life.

That kind of soil only comes when we give our hearts to God entirely, totally, and completely. We need to determine that through God's help and our commitment, we will not allow the enemy of our souls to snatch away His seed over our fields. We will allow God's Word the time it needs to sink in deeply and not be scorched by heat. We will make it a daily habit of life to remove the things in our field that hinder its growth.

Good, fertile soil does not appear all by itself. The Gardener changes the soil.

We need people in our lives who know how to raise our arms up when we're weary, like Aaron and Hurr, without recognition or a pat on the back. Our number of faithful warriors doesn't have to be big. Last time I checked, we only have two arms. These warriors don't need war paint on their cheeks for everyone to see. They are the ones with blistered hands who never let go.

We need to read our Bible every day, even if we don't remember what we read yesterday. What we feed grows even when we don't see it yet. There is a meditation of holiness that quenches every thirst we have before we ever knew we were thirsty. It's water for our soul.

We need to command our soul to praise the Lord even when we don't feel it. If we wait for our flesh to align with our spirit, then we will only be a seasonal worshipper dictated by how we feel. Seasonal worshippers don't produce 30, 60, or 100-fold.

We need to sit still in His presence. Sometimes that is all we can do. This helps develop Holy Spirit wisdom and discernment. We are people that want to know "why." Knowing why doesn't set us free. Knowing the truth sets us free. God is the way, the TRUTH, and the life. The only way to know the truth is to spend time with the One who is.

In our humanness, silence makes us believe that nothing is happening. In our holiness, we realize that silence allows for the most to happen. We have to refuse to meditate on our traumas. Instead, we need to meditate on the truth.

Jesus wants us to be productive in our service to His Kingdom. He is always scattering His good seed into the soil of our fields. The harvest and flourishing are abundant for the one whose life is fully yielded to Him. This is the soil that develops the deep root system, receives the nourishment, and bears fruit. They hear and receive. This is an element of believing. This is an act of the will where we choose to receive what He has for us. We choose to receive the pathway to growing and bearing fruit.

Do we have a receptive heart?

Do we make space for Him in our daily living?

Do we believe what He says?

Are we able to be corrected?

Do we really want what He has for us–even if we don't like the methods He uses?

I want to trust the Gardener in such a way that I am ready to receive the gift of how He comes.

Jesus tells us in the parable of the good soil that the one who hears the Word and receives it is the one who produces a crop yielding a hundred, sixty, or thirty-fold. In ancient Israel, it would have been nearly impossible for a farmer to receive a return that was more than 10-fold. When Jesus offers us 100-fold, He is talking about a return that is unheard of. God is a generous giver. He isn't limited by resources or knowledge. When He rewards, He rewards well.

The problem isn't with the sower. The problem isn't with the seed. The problem isn't with God's word. The problem is with the soil. The problem is with the receptiveness of the human heart. Depending on how receptive it is, the soil of our hearts can bring about lasting joy in our lives.

Our inability to produce 100-fold is not on the sower who promised it to us. We have a responsibility and a part to play if we want to experience 100-fold. Friends, it's not out of reach. Not even close. It awaits us all if we will hear and receive.

REFLECT

- How does it make you feel to know that the love of God sows seed onto your soil even when your soil isn't good?
- Is your impatient, spiritual stomach binging on junk food? How does it affect your appetite for all that God is offering in the nourishing?
- Do you want to be a receiver of His Word and the scattering of His Seed?
- What practical steps can you take today to have a more receptive heart?

SCRIPTURE

> The seed falling on good soil refers to someone who hears the word and understands it. This is the one who produces a crop, yielding a hundred, sixty, or thirty times what was sown.
>
> Mark 4:20

PRAYER

Heavenly Father, I want to be the good soil, the one who hears the Word, absorbs its worth, and brings forth an abundance of fruit because of it. I want 100-fold lasting fruit: love, joy, peace, patience, kindness, goodness, faithfulness, gentleness, and self-control. Time spent in Your Word, Your presence, and in worship produces godliness in me. I want to be faithful in my part of bringing about 100-fold. Help me to have a receptive heart to Your Word. In Jesus' name, amen.

We try to keep it tidy,
We primp and we clean.
We slap some lipstick on the pig,
Of the rotting that's within.

Hardened and alone,
We get used to the weight.
Distractions, rocks, and thorns choke out,
As bondage becomes our fate.

We're enticed to desires,
To fill a void that won't stay filled.
Until we hear a voice that asks,
"Do you want to be made well?"

A transplant of our spirit,
Is what we really need.
I've tried all the other sources,
But now only Jesus do I seek.

May we stop trading abundance,
For plates of emptiness.
Because you can't weather the storms of life,
If you don't have the depth.

Prepare the ground of your heart,
Let your roots deeply grow.
As you weapon with your worship,
So He can cultivate the soil.

PART THREE

Pruning

To cut away dead or overgrown branches to increase fruitfulness and growth.

CHAPTER TWELVE

Renaming the Soil

The seed falling on good soil refers to someone who hears the word and understands it. This is the one who produces a crop, yielding a hundred, sixty, or thirty times what was sown.
Mark 4:20

Oftentimes, loss goes hand-in-hand with gain. They seem to hold hands. With one comes the other. The death of one thing is often required for the birth of something beautiful and new. The end of one thing is the beginning of something different–something special. It's the beginning of something so bright and fresh and lovely.

We have a hard time letting things go.

We have a hard time accepting the endings.

We have a hard time coming to terms with losses of all kinds.

If only we knew what was coming.

If only we knew what God was birthing in the death of "what was."

If only we knew that what God was using for our gain is so much more beautiful than any of the things that are passing away.

There's beauty in it all. He uses it all.

Pruning is the journey to fruitfulness. There's an inability to experience fruitfulness in our lives without also experiencing pruning.

If you have followed Jesus for very long, you've experienced pruning. There's a great likelihood that He's begun cutting away things in your life that don't look like Him. If that process has not begun yet, it will.

It is imperative that we see value in having our minds fixed on things above. His word in Philippians 4:8 tells us:

> Whatever things are true, honorable, right, pure, lovely, admirable—if anything is excellent and worthy of praise—think on these things.

Friends, we can all survive the seasons of pruning in our lives and be better for it. However, it won't be a very enjoyable ride if our minds and hearts aren't focused on things above. You may get to where you're going, but you won't see the value in the scenery along the way. There is a verse that has held me during pruning seasons:

> Rejoice always, pray continually, give thanks in all circumstances; for this is God's will for you in Christ Jesus.
> 1 Thessalonians 5:18

We must know how to implement this verse in our lives during the pruning seasons. If we believe that God's will for our lives won't include earthly pain, tribulation, and discomfort, we won't know how to rejoice when they come. God's will for our lives isn't about what we *do*; it's about who we are *becoming*. When we can learn how to thank Him when circumstances don't seem fair and when life feels brutal, we become like Jesus. Becoming like Jesus and bearing His image is God's will for our lives. That is only possible through pruning.

In the growth segment, we learned about how Esau's birthright and inheritance were traded to his younger brother Jacob for a bowl of beans. Their father, Isaac, blind and on his deathbed, desired to give his final blessing to Esau. However, Jacob posed as Esau and received the family blessing instead. When Esau realized what had happened and came to his senses, rage set in. It is in this very moment of rage that Esau declares his intentions to murder his brother Jacob. This leads to the climactic scene in Genesis 28 where Jacob fled from his brother's hatred.

It is in this pivotal piece of the story where God encountered Jacob in his running.

> Jacob left Beersheba and set out for Harran. When He reached a certain place, he stopped for the night because the sun had set. Taking one of the stones there, he put it under his head and lay down to sleep. He had a dream. There the Lord said, "I am the Lord, the God of your father Abraham and the God of Isaac. I will give you and your descendants this land. All people will be blessed through you and your offspring. I am with you and will watch over you wherever you go, and I will bring you back to this land. I will not leave you until I have done what I have promised.
> Pieces from Genesis 28

God gave Esau, as the firstborn, the opportunity to receive his inheritance. God knew the person that Esau would grow to become, and He also knew all that Jacob would grow to become. They were drastically different.

Jacob was flawed, but he was faithful. His story mirrors the life of nearly every believer: imperfect, at times full of earthly sorrow, but with hope in the end. Suffering builds character and allows us to grow closer to Him, as we realize that there is nothing to be valued above Him. Had Jacob been the firstborn, the promise would have come more easily to him, and he wouldn't have had to face trial after trial the way that he did. The suffering made him like Jesus. It is what propelled him to have a mind molded like Jesus.

Just because we inherit a blessing doesn't mean there won't be persecution. Jesus tells us in John 16:33, "In this life you will have trouble, but take heart. I have overcome the world." Even with peace in God, there will be tribulation in our days. Even knowing there is victory through Jesus, we will experience tribulation and hardships.

We must learn the importance of pressing into Him, through praise and worship, even when we don't feel it. We can make our current happenings an idol if we aren't careful. The danger occurs when our circumstances take a nosedive. We are left not knowing how to respond with joy. Giving thanks in *all* circumstances offers us unshakable contentment through Him. When we can learn to give thanks in all circumstances, we learn to praise Him because of who He is, not what He is giving.

There will be hardship, friends. We have to pre-decide how we are going to respond to it.

No better than an exile, Jacob fled to this foreign place. This feels a lot like us sometimes, fleeing the moment things get hard. Running in an attempt to abandon all of the chaos. The minute there's resistance in our lives, we buckle, right?

Jacob consistently approached his circumstances with fear and doubt. We, too, can have shaky knees and a quivering faith. Even still, God pressed in and used Jacob through his weaknesses. These trials shaped Jacob, and his character was formed from them.

Tribulations in our lives are not indicators that something is wrong. Instead, tribulations in our lives allow God to meet with us. Tribulations in our lives open the door for revelation, breakthrough, and refinement.

While Jacob, in his distress, was fleeing from his homeland to escape his brother's plot to kill him, he spent the night sleeping with his head on a rock. Mid-journey, at a site chosen because of nightfall, he stopped to sleep. As he slept, God appeared to him in a vision. His dream disclosed the hidden yet active presence of God. Even in Jacob's imperfect and disrupted life, God engaged.

Even in our imperfect, disrupted, messy, and broken lives, God engages.

In this moment, God appeared to Jacob not when Jacob was royalty or even a priest but rather to Jacob when he was a terrified refugee. God appeared to a broken man in shattered circumstances. It's all messy–every part of it. In this intimate and personal encounter, God passed along to Jacob all the promises given to Abraham. God chose this moment to reveal every promise that He had for Jacob. He chose this moment! God brought such sweet assurance to Jacob.

It is at this very moment when Jacob literally renamed this place. Jacob was so convinced of the holiness of the place where the Lord visited him that night that he made the decision and declaration to rename the space from Luz (light) to Bethel, which means House of God.

We aren't promised a life without hardship. But we are promised that He will never lead us outside of His light. It was His light shining in the darkness that allowed Jacob to rename this place!

The night Jacob laid his head upon that rock became a marker in his life. It became the place where God met with Him. It was the place where He was anointed by God. In one of the most distressing, terrifying, and lonely spaces that Jacob had ever found himself in, it was the exact place that became a marker in his life of revelation, assurance, and promise.

There are a multitude of takeaways from this story and how it relates to the pruning season of our lives–too many to graft into one singular book. That being said, here are some main promises and takeaways that I hold close:

- **God can and will meet us in foreign, unexpected places.** He met Jacob while he was in distress. He met with Jacob while Jacob was on the run. He met Jacob while his head was on a rock–on a hard thing. Ordinary people in the middle of a mess are sometimes the means for God's widespread blessing.
- **He is with us wherever we go.** There is no place outside of His scope.
- **When God comes in close, He always brings assurance.**
- **God wants all of us.** He wants us to surrender our lives to Him. This is the gateway to making our hearts His home.
- **We need to rename some places, spaces, circumstances & seasons.** It doesn't have to be called what it's always been called. It doesn't have to be called what it feels/looks like.

What if every space we entered, every place we encountered, every circumstance and season we found ourselves in was renamed to Bethel, House of God?

We have cursed the ground around us long enough. It's time to rename that soil! Our encounters with the Holy God, even in this pruning season, should become "markers" for those who come after us, for our children and our children's children. This "anointed rock" where Jacob laid his head became the place for Israel where God meets with His people.

Remember: hard places in our lives are not indicators of something gone wrong, they are places where God brings revelation and promises.

Could this pruning season be renamed? Is it possible that this painful place could be the very space that becomes a "marker" in your life, one filled with revelation, assurance, and promise? It could become the very place that creates the space for you to meet with God in your surrender.

I've heard it said that "comfort is the god of our generation." This is exactly why we become so frustrated with verses like Romans 8:28:

> We know that in all things God works for the good
> of those who love Him, who have been called according
> to His purpose.

How can this be so? How can God work all things together for our good? All things? I don't know about you, but I've endured some things that didn't feel very good. Worse, they were excruciatingly painful.

What's "your thing?"

Be honest right now. What's your thing that feels so incredibly painful in your life?

What's the thing that feels like a thorn in your flesh?

What's the thing that you wish would go away?

Something that God had to change and heal in me was my expectation. Disappointment had become my emotional home for so many years. My "thing" was enduring harsh realities at the hands of people who I thought should look more like Jesus and didn't. My "thing" has not made my life more comfortable, quite the contrary. My expectations of others set me in a snare. I trapped myself right into the deceiver's disappointment each time.

My thing looked like a dead end.

My thing led me through deep valleys.

My thing was long-lasting.

I allowed my thing to suck hope and joy out of me.

My thing made me ache in pain and devastation.

I began to learn that I couldn't receive the abundance of what God had *presently* for me if I was living in past pain. I had to come to this place, over and over again, where I chose not to let the hurt I'm experiencing doubt the purpose that I carry.

I'll say it again. Do not allow the hurt you are experiencing make you doubt the purpose you carry!

If we define "good" as equating to what's comfortable, we will forever live in stagnancy, pain, and frustration. Thankfully, Paul keeps writing. In Romans 8:29, Paul tells us that the pathway that leads us into deeper likeness to Jesus involves and includes our "thing."

> For those He foreknew, He also predestined to be conformed to the image of His son.

God's definition of good is different from ours. Our definition of good is comfortable, rich, successful, easy. However, Paul says our "thing" will make us more like Jesus. Becoming more like Jesus is the very thing that we look at and become boggled by. The means to deep transformation isn't what we would think. It's clothed in humility and surrender.

The agent to becoming more like Jesus involves the things we are enduring and think, "How could this even be used for good?"

Even if that "thing" makes you feel weak, He wants to use it. Even if you'd never choose it, stop doubting that He can. Stay open to what God is doing in the waiting. If you want to silence the enemy in this pruning season, stay there. If you want to shut up the enemy in this pruning season, stand there. Do you want to overcome the feelings of doubt and hopelessness to experience the joy of the Lord? Stand there.

Maybe some of the stuff you are dealing with in your life doesn't need to be shrunk down. Maybe you need to be pruned and then raised up!

You can be in undesirable soil and sprout there. You can be in undesirable soil and bloom there. You can be clipped by the Master's Hand and flourish there. You can be in devastating pain, running from all of your troubles in the wilderness, and God can meet you right there.

The wilderness can be the place of God's provision. The wilderness can be the place that leads us to depend upon God. The wilderness can be the place where we discover that He is the only One who can fill and satisfy. The wilderness can be the place that reveals the lack of all lesser loves.

Pruning is the agent to knowing Jesus more. Pruning is the agent to refinement. Pruning is the agent to deeper purity. He may be pruning you in what feels like a wilderness season. Hold fast.

You can be in undesirable soil and sprout there. You can be in undesirable soil and bloom there. You can be clipped by the Master's Hand and flourish there.

REFLECT

- Is there an area of your life that you have found yourself fleeing from?
- Is there an area of your life where you feel distressed?
- In these areas of distress, what are your thoughts centered around? Where is your fix of focus in moments and seasons of distress? Are your thoughts centered around anxiousness, worry, fear, doubt? Or are you diligently thinking about these things: whatever is true, honest, just, pure, lovely, admirable, excellent, worthy of praise.

Take some time and journal about where God has you. Be intentional in writing out praise worthy aspects of the journey where He has you. You are the apple of His eye. Let's activate our faith muscle and trust that God knows what He is doing. He is working under the soil and behind the scenes!

SCRIPTURE

> In a desert land He found Him, in a barren and howling waste. He shielded him and cared for him; He guarded him as the apple of His eye.
>
> Deuteronomy 32:10

PRAYER

Lord, I come to You today with open hands and an open heart. The struggles that surround me in this season weigh heavily on me. Through every trial and hardship, You are good. Grant me understanding when the outcome isn't what I want it to be. Remind me that Your plans are better for me than my own. Open my eyes to Your provision as You help me surrender control. Provide me with strength to endure all that is yet to come. When I am full of doubt, show me Your hand at work. When I am scared, grow my faith bigger than my fear. When I am disheartened, guide me to seek You in my pain. When it feels like too much, let Your presence feel near. Lord, You came that I may have life and have it full. Direct me to live it out in abundance.

CHAPTER THIRTEEN
Abiding

Each year, I clear out the remnants of tomato plants in my garden from the previous summer. The once strong, lively, and sturdy green limbs withered over the winter. The brown remains that were dry and dead nearly dissolved as I began pulling them out. That's the thing about branches. Once they dry and wither, they have no purpose. A dead tree can be used for so many other things. Entire houses can be built with their remains. However, they have no strength when it's detached from its source. It's only good for burning.

Jesus used this imagery to explain what we become when we fail to abide in Him. He told his disciples on the eve of His death:

> I am the vine; you are the branches. Whoever
> abides in me and I in him, he bears much fruit, for apart
> from me you can do nothing. If anyone does not abide
> in me he is thrown away like a branch and withers; and
> the branches are gathered, thrown into the fire, and
> burned. If you abide in me, and my words abide in you,
> ask whatever you wish, and it will be done for you. By
> this my Father is glorified, that you bear much fruit and
> so prove to be my disciples.
> John 15:5-8

Jesus warns us that apart from Him, we can do nothing. On our own, we are completely devoid of effectiveness and strength. We need His eternal source to have abundant and continual fruit.

Our life's purpose should be to build a life centered on our relationship with Jesus. Everything is an overflow of that relationship. Growth happens when we make time for Him, each and every day. To meet with Him in His Word, meditating on it day and night. To truly grasp our need to, like David, pant for His presence and to desire to take Him in like water for our thirsty souls.

While the world seeks to conform us to its pattern, Jesus seeks to transform us by renewing our minds.

Abiding not only renews our minds; it transforms our desires. We begin to seek more out of life. We want His name to be glorified, His will to be done, His kingdom to come. Our hope is no longer in what we can gain but in what we can bear—to bear much fruit, not for our own glory, but to glorify God in all we do. Our whole perspective will change when we depend upon Christ continually. We will begin to see His handprints in even the smallest things.

A precious mentor shared this picture of a tree right outside her house with me one day. It was captivating.

The image of this snapped tree is the image of us. We are not promised that there will not be breakage that occurs in the environments of this world. Things will happen—even when we have a strong root system. Hard things will come upon us and there will be complete breakage and suffering.

However, God is a God of mercy, and He will not allow us to be destroyed completely. He won't.

Initially, what you may see when you look at that snapped tree is brokenness, bareness, and a posture that is hunched over by the weight of what is holding it down. But if you take a deeper look, you will also see life. They can coexist and oftentimes do.

God always allows the breaking before the blessing. If not, we'd be unchanged, selfish, and demanding.

God always allows the crushing before we step into our calling. If not, we would step into assignments with a haughty spirit that seeks to gratify the self.

God always allows the pressing before the prize. If not, we'd hold the prize with hands and hearts that were ungrateful.

The Kingdom of God can feel like it works backwards. It does. What may feel like destruction and breakage is His Holy preparation. God uses the breakage to shape us and help us to steward what He has for us. We are the branches that must stay connected to Him in order to receive the nutrients, nourishment, and care that He can offer us.

> I am the true vine, and my Father is the gardener. He
> lifts up/cuts off (aeri) every branch in Me that does not
> bear fruit, while every branch that does bear fruit He
> prunes so that it will be even more fruitful. If you remain
> in Me and I in you, you will bear much fruit; apart from
> Me you can do nothing.
> John 15:1-2, 5

When Jeremy and I had our first son, Hunter, the hospital gave us a gift card to a local nursery to pick out an apple tree. We were so excited to get the tree home and planted. We were so excited the following summer to see small little green apples sprouting off the limb. The tree was so fragile. Not once, but twice, we ran over this apple tree with the lawnmower and flattened it to the ground.

I looked outside one afternoon and saw Jeremy taking three stakes and driving them into the ground. He secured the tree upright with some twine that he found in the garage.

The seasons came and went. A couple of years later, our son, Hunter, ran inside and said, "Mom! You'll never guess! The apple tree has leaves!"

I ran outside and sure enough, it had leaves.

I heard Rick Warren say one time, "In God's garden of grace, even a broken tree can bear fruit."

That day was pivotal for me. I can vividly remember seeing Jeremy kneeling down, taking that fallen, broken apple tree in his hands, standing it up, and securing it. God does exactly that.

One quick assessment of a good gardener is that they will stake down an anchor next to a broken limb, attach the weighted limb to the stake, and give it security through the process of lifting it up off the ground. Look at that picture of the snapped tree. There is a stake that offers structural support that eventually leads to new life and new growth.

When His Word references the branches that do not bear fruit for Him, the Hebrew word is *aeri*. *Aeri* literally means to lift up. The first move of God in our breakage and lack is to lift us up closer to Himself so that we can draw from the source of all that we need from Him.

He doesn't immediately cut us off like a man does. He doesn't cut us off without first offering us the ability to know Him more deeply through abiding. He knows that if we stay close to Him when the winds come, when the storms rage around us, when the environments are harsh, that we will have all that we need from Him. He knows that if we abide in Him, we will be able to bear fruit for His name.

We can be blessed from God's perspective and not feel blessed from our perspective.

His Word goes on to say that the branches that are already bearing fruit, He prunes so that they can bear even more fruit. He rewards those who bear fruit for Him. He desires to give us more fruit. Now, the *process* of more fruit may not be what you or I would choose, but if it is the method of God, I know there's no greater way.

Pruning is a painful process of cutting back dead and overgrown things in our lives. Many of us know it is a painful process and often a less-than-glamorous initial viewing. It can look really gory at first.

I vividly remember coming home from work one day, pulling in the driveway, and seeing my poor rose bush! What in the world happened to it?! It looked so bare! I ran inside and asked my husband if he knew what happened. He explained that a lot of the branches had died and become overgrown, and that he needed to cut them back so that they would be able to bloom more fully next year.

Next year?

What about the rest of this year?!

They are just going to look like they'd been through the weedwacker until next spring?

Spiritually, we can be vain like this in our walk with the Lord sometimes, too. We can become more mesmerized by the external things that God is doing for us that we disregard the value of the inward work. When we don't fully trust Him, we can desire the appearance of lusciousness, even if the limbs are on the verge of death. We can prefer to have areas of our lives be overgrown and living in lack rather than allowing the Master Gardener to clip so that we can yield a bounty of abundance in times to come.

Is it because we know that the clipping will hurt?

Or is it because we don't want to give up what has become familiar for something new that we can't yet see or understand?

Could it be because surrendering to His pruning would require us to change and become different?

It may be a combination of all, even.

We can be miserable, dragging around those dead things in our lives, or we can surrender and allow God to prune them away.

Over the years of my Babylon, God pruned me in so many ways. Dead limbs were lying all around me, as He clipped, that I didn't even realize were weighing me down and making me less than fruitful. I came to a place in my walk with the Lord where I knew that the only way for me to be free from all the pain that I was enduring was to allow Him to do a deep work in me. My heart's desire was to become more like Him and to become less like me. I asked Him to show me areas that weren't fruitful. I asked Him to reveal the hidden places that were corrupt—the places that only He could see. I began allowing Him to clip away at every idol thing in my life.

Our dead and overgrown branches will all have different names. These were some of mine: hate, jealousy, envy, bitterness, discontentment, selfishness, stubbornness, a controlling spirit.

That is a lot of dead limbs, let me tell you!

You don't realize how many there are until you begin seeing yourself without them. You begin to wonder how you ever dragged all of them around.

In John 12:25, Jesus speaks these words:

> Unless a kernel of wheat falls to the ground and dies, it remains only a single seed. But if it dies, it produces many seeds. Anyone who loves their life will lose it, while anyone who hates their life in this world, will keep it for eternal life.

Seeds have to die in order for something new to come from them. We must, too. If we will submit ourselves to His planting and His pruning, there will be new life that flourishes forth. In order to live, we must die to ourselves and to everything that doesn't look like Him. If we want to experience and share in the resurrecting power of Jesus Christ, we must be willing to share in suffering, becoming like Him in death. The death of ourselves is a necessary agent in looking more like Jesus. We are only ever going to get to know the power of His resurrection to the degree to which we are willing to die to ourselves.

When I say that He calls us to die to ourselves, I am referring to the surrender of allowing God to kill everything in our lives that doesn't bear the fruit of His name. Oftentimes, this requires us to kill our own will and wants. If the branch doesn't bear fruit of love, joy, peace, patience, kindness, goodness, faithfulness, gentleness, or self-control in our lives, then it needs to die.

I had to put to death hate above all things. That was the heaviest of dead limbs in my life. The enemy had allowed me to feel justified in my hate based on the depths of pain that had happened in my life. However, the fruit of God's word says to bless those who curse you and pray for those who have mistreated you. I had to cut out hate to bear the fruit of love.

Let me again encourage you in this grace-filled truth:

Letting go of all of the dead limbs is a process and it is a journey. It is also a reward!!

The biblical term for this is sanctification. The Hebrew word for sanctification in the Bible is "qadash," meaning to set apart as holy. It is the process of being freed from sin and bondage and being purified and made holy. It's what He desires for our lives so that we can experience abundant living through Him. It takes time, obedience, and staying close to Him.

Sanctification is not the process of being set apart just for the sake of being separated. Romans 1:1 says that we are separated UNTO God. The Greek Word for "set apart" is actually "aphorizo," which means to be set off by a boundary, to appoint, to sever. Biblically, it is used to mark off.

God knows what severing in our lives needs to be severed. He is doing this so that there is room for Him to add all that He has for us. Sanctification is the process by which God separates us from our old lives. We aren't the people we used to be. We have been set aside for a special purpose. We have been reserved for the use of the Master Gardener at His appointed time.

There will never be a time in your walk with the Lord when you won't need to undergo the pruning cut from the Master Gardener's Hand. There will never be a time when you won't be undergoing the sanctification process. Becoming holy is a process, and it is one that should feel like the highest privilege.

I can't imagine someone looking nothing like me and yet going around and telling people that they belong to me. However, we do it all the time through the name of Jesus. We tell people that we love Him and we bear His name, and sometimes we don't look anything like Him.

Our desire should be to stand underneath the clip of the Master Gardener's Hand so that we never stop looking like Him. Every cut turns us into a greater likeness of His image.

Every cut holds purpose.

Every cut holds promise.

Every cut produces a deeper flourishing.

That is a really humbling and privilege-filled anointing to regard and carry.

Allowing God to cut away at our heart represents our obedience, love and loyalty to trust Him with the deepest, most tender parts. It represents commitment. Do not get discouraged in the process. There will be times when you don't always bear the fruit that you should because you aren't staying attached to Him through His Word, prayer, and praise. This is simply an identifier of additional overgrown and dead branches, in which you can invite Him to prune.

Even when we are walking in obedience, it can be a brutal and ugly process. Refer back to the image of the staked tree. There are times when my heart is ugly, impatient, unkind, envious, boastful, arrogant, and rude. In these seasons of pruning, there are times when I insist on my own way. In 1 Corinthians 13:7, Paul, the same guy who was set apart *unto* God's purposes, the same guy who taught us how to allow the hard things in our lives make us more like Jesus, tells us this:

> Love bears all things, believes all things, hopes all things and endures all things."

In the most painful of my Babylon season, I didn't always bear, believe, hope for, or endure all things well. I was the opposite of loving. I was hateful, often. I was ungrateful. I was the disobedient Israelite. I didn't embrace and love the seasons that felt crushing. I didn't always believe that God was using it for my good. I didn't always have hope. I sure didn't endure any of it joyfully.

However, there were pivotal moments where I made the declaration that I didn't want to be cursed to roam the desert and never see the Promised Land. I wanted to walk into the fullness of His promises. So, I chose to allow Him to cut away hate.

Staying close to Him is the key. Trusting Him when logic is screaming that nothing is changing is the key. The pathway to looking more like Jesus and looking less like yourself is abiding: remaining, staying attached to Him.

Friend, you can't muster up a "new you" on your own. You can't strive your way into looking like Jesus. You can't do it on your own. Apart from Him, you can do nothing.

Allowing God to cut away at our heart represents our obedience, love and loyalty to trust Him with the deepest and most tender parts.

We are called to bear fruit, not produce it. There's a difference.

Producing fruit requires a striving pursuit.

Bearing fruit is an abiding nature.

A fruit tree doesn't live in a stressed posture, striving to grow fruit. It stays rooted. It takes in sunlight. It draws nutrients from the soil. In time,  fruit will grow. The same thing is so for us. Forcing ourselves to produce fruit will never work. We must stay connected to Jesus in the Vine to bear fruit. Flourishing through Jesus takes work and discipline. But we don't work for God; we work from Him.

If you stay close to Him, even if it feels like the wilderness, even if it feels like you are "out of season," even if it feels like no one else is with you but Him, even if it feels insurmountable, you will reap a flourishing harvest that is bigger than anything you could dream or imagine.

One night, my daughter watched as the sun began to set over us. She quickly positioned herself underneath the beams and radiance of the setting sun and said, "Look, Mommy. I'm standing right under the sun."

And she was. At that moment, she was the most beautiful she'd ever been.

Just like the sun, His presence is always moving.

> **Draw near to God, and He will draw near to you.**
> James 4:7

If you don't meditate on the promises of God for your spiritual maturation and encouragement, you are truly missing out on some of the most blessed aspects of your relationship with the Lord. There are immeasurable promises that hold me in hard times, but this one, this promise, stands above so many others. There's just something so comforting in knowing that if we will take a step towards Him, He will step towards us, too. If we will remain in Him, He will remain in us. He doesn't force us to abide. However, He will stay as close to us as we are willing to stay to Him.

Abiding provides the provision for all that we could ever need.

Several years ago, I decided that I wanted to start some plants, herbs, and flowers from seed that year. As soon as I got them all planted, I knew I needed to get them some sun. I did some research and quickly realized that I needed a shelf or riser so that they would receive sunlight directly.

We are the same.

Proximity to His presence becomes the gateway to growth.

It's where we are positioned that decides whether we will grow or not. When we position ourselves close to His SON, Jesus, seeds will spring forth from the fertile soil of our hearts. We get to partner with Him in the depths and magnitude of what He wants to do in and through us. The spiritual shelf that positions us closer to Him is the desire of our heart to pursue Him, to seek Him. It's the method of surrendering all things to Him.

I want to be in the light as He is in the light.

I want seeds to spring up that honor Him, that reflect His nature, that glorify Him.

Proximity is the answer. The power of His presence is what changes us. It's what compels us to holy living. Proximity is what allows for us to be close to the clip of the Master Gardener's hand.

Position yourself close to the Son and watch as He begins to transform you! You will never be more beautiful than when you are nearest to Him. You will never bear more fruit than when you are attached to Him. There is a flourishing that is on the horizon.

Proximity to His presence becomes the provision for everything you face and everything you will ever need.

REFLECT

- What are the names of your dead limbs?
- What areas of your heart does God need to continue to cut away and prune?
- How can you trust Him more fully in the clipping and pruning?
- What are practical ways that you can position yourself closer to Him in this season?

SCRIPTURE

> The Lord your God will circumcise (cut away) your heart so that you may love Him with all your soul and live.
> Deuteronomy 30:6

PRAYER

Lord, I commit myself to Your pruning process. I ask for grace to willingly let go of the things that don't bear fruit in my lie—even when it is difficult. Help me to surrender fully to Your will, trusting that You know what is best for me. Shape and direct me so that I can be fruitful in every area of my life. I desire to stay close to You so that I can bear fruit that lasts.

CHAPTER FOURTEEN

The God Who Sees

I believe that there is nothing more essential in this pruning season than believing that God sees us. When we lose sight of that, hopelessness begins to wreak havoc in our minds. We have to believe and trust that He is with us as we allow Him to let go of all that needs gone.

It's not easy. But it's worth it.

We either believe that He is Immanuel, God with us, or He's not. Trusting that He sees us and is with us in the painful and refining process is absolutely vital.

I've mentored and discipled a lot of women over the years. Do you know what the #1 most common reason I've observed as to why they stop trusting God? They stop trusting God in seasons of hardship when they feel like they are being tested. What's worse than being in a season of testing, is being in a season of testing that is taking longer than you thought or wanted it to.

When we think of tests, it is not uncommon for many of us to think of performance or failure. Friends, that is not God's purpose through the testing. It is not perfection that He wants. It's purification that He desires.

God's goal in the testing is deeper roots, greater growth, more fruit, and a character that looks more like Him. We allow tests to make us believe that they are all negative in nature. To God, they aren't failure seasons! When God tests us, good things can happen!

God is healing us in our pruning seasons. It may not be how we want Him to, though. Oftentimes, we want the end result of what the pruning offers, but we don't want what it feels like to get there.

Pruning removes unwanted branches and improves our structure, much like pruning does for plants and trees. It also encourages flourishing growth. If we want to flourish, we have to be open to letting go of what holds us back. He is the Master Gardener, and He is faithful to return each morning with care. He knows the kind of fruit that we can bear if we surrender to Him. Everything that was cut back will one day thrive. His desire is for us to flourish and bear fruit–even in old age. His pruning is a reminder to us of the intentional and tender care that He takes in leading us towards greater growth and deeper depths.

Our hearts are an unending project for the Lord. I'm thankful for that. I'm thankful that there is always deeper purity to be obtained, and yet, there are times when I run from the pruning, forgetting that the Gardener knows the deeper the cutting and trimming, the richer the cluster that can grow.

In one of the most severe pruning seasons of my life, I know that I would've never survived it without the faith to believe that He saw me in it. In painful seasons, we can begin forming our own "truths." These "truths" are usually filled with personal opinions and assumptions. They are chasms away from His truth.

My "truth" during a harsh season was flooded with rejection that was rooted in wrong security. It was causing unrest in my mind, confusion, ugly and brutal realities. There were wrong deposits being placed into my soil that were affecting my marriage, my role as a mother, my effectiveness as a friend, and the intimacy of my relationship with Jesus.

As a means for validation and acceptance, perhaps even an attempt to be seen, I had enlisted myself in every aspect of church ministry to seek connection, identity, purpose, and inclusion. At one point in time, I was in six different ministries at church. Even thinking about this now feels really exhausting and humiliating.

Ministry is this weird phenomenon where many step into it for reasons that aren't entirely wrong, and yet, over time, everything about it becomes wrong. It's this slow fade that is almost unrecognizable. It happens through small movements, the little choices, the need for more: more control, more applause, more praise, and more adoration. It becomes like a shot of heroin in our veins. It inflates every part of us that feels empty.

Before long, we are sourced through validation, the accolades, and the praises of man. That leads to a need to be filled by that source over and over again. We find ourselves standing at the well of man's acceptance with our bucket in hand. We become content with our thirst being satisfied by this water. This water is refreshing at first, but it parches us in seconds and leaves us standing at the base of the well where we don't feel like we can leave even if we know we need to. The thirst is too severe. Our tongues are sticking to the roof of our mouths, and we become dependent upon it.

We all have found ourselves reaching for a counterfeit identity.

We each have found ourselves searching for fruitless attempts to find meaning.

Your "truths," personal opinions and assumptions may be different from mine. Yet, they will lead you wrongly all the same.

The wrong vine will attach you to the wrong things and bear the wrong fruit. Just because something is good doesn't mean that it is good for *you*. We must be held by the true Vine and led by His Spirit. When we are led by everything but Christ, anything that blows our way feels like a temptation. Our insecurities will force us into places and positions that aren't His will for us. For me, they led me to good things for bad reasons. The right things can be wrong when our hearts are sick.

If the well we are standing in front of isn't His living water, it's just a barren well.

Your barren well will look different than mine. That much is true, but it all leads us to the same place. We all are in need of His living water and pruning shears in order to receive Him fully.

An aspect of pruning in my life that felt really painful was when God began clipping these ministries away. Over time, many were clipped away completely. As I look back now, I can see the hand of God over my life in each and every closed door, cutting away everything that wasn't fruitful. Tearing down and uprooting every idol. An idol can be anything that you worship outside of God. It is anything that takes up more time, adoration, and attention than Jesus. It is anything that draws our attention away from Him. Good things can become idols in our lives. Church things can become idols. They can.

Every door that God closes is His will for our lives. Every clipping by His hand is His mercy and grace. Every idol will keep us from the secret place of abiding with Him. Anything that we hold closer than Him is the enemy's snare for us. Anything that we attach ourselves to aside from Him will result in the wrong things, no matter how tempting it looks.

At some point, we have to get sick of drinking from wells that don't satisfy.

We have to get sick of drawing from places that leave us more thirsty than when we first came. At some point, we have to be done standing on the brink of barren resources.

Oftentimes, those wells end up being mirages. They are optical phenomena where what you are looking at appears to be real, but it's not actually there. It is just an illusion. Mirages appear in the desert places. They appear when we are most thirsty. They can be deceiving. Mirages make us see things that aren't really there. They can make you believe that if you drink from them, you will be fulfilled, but it's just a mirage.

When we are spiritually in the hot, desert season, mirages look so inviting.

When the roofs of our spiritual mouths are dry and cracking, they make us believe that our thirst will be quenched.

All that's really there when we get there is more dryness. We keep walking towards them, and nothing is ever there. If we aren't careful, we can find ourselves pursuing mirages instead of pursuing Him.

When we are peering through faulty lenses, everything is distorted. I can see that now. However, all those years ago, it felt imperative to all that I thought I needed.

There's a magnified difference between set aside and being SET APART.

One is a lie. The other is truth.

His truth says this:

> You have been set apart as holy to the Lord your God,
> and He has chosen you to be His own special treasure.
>
> Deuteronomy 14:2

If there's one thing I want you to hear from this entire book, it is this: You are set apart! You are. Oftentimes the process of being set apart is something we don't welcome easily and don't fully understand. However, it doesn't mean that it's not the best that He has for us.

I was on a walk around a nearby town one day, looking at tulips, when I became captivated by a single stem in a sea of fuchsia.

One single stem of yellow planted in the very center of a field of nothing like it. Look, I know flowers don't have feelings, but often I like to let my mind imagine and tell stories. I just wonder, if flowers could feel, how would this single yellow stem feel?

Would it feel out of place?

Would it feel like it didn't belong?

Would it feel like it got planted in the wrong soil?

Or would it feel the treasure of being set apart?

Are the patterns of our mind ones catapulted by, "I'm rejected, and I don't belong," rather than, "I'm set apart as a treasure for Him to use."

Regardless, I do believe that there will be aspects of this earthly walk with Jesus that can feel very lonely. You'll encounter loneliness as you seek to be set apart for His purposes.

You will.

That's true, but as you are obedient to take steps towards deeper holiness in Him, you will encounter the most amazing people who are on this set-apart journey with you, and it's going to lead to some of the most abundant and flourishing relationships you could've ever imagined. You just have to trust what you cannot see.

God sees us in our hurt. He sees our ache. He sees our longings. He sees it all. He doesn't disregard it. He takes us deeper so that we can experience the fullness of freedom through His healing. There are depths of rich soil that await!

One of the deepest pruning cuts from the Lord came when it felt like so much was being stripped already. Through His pruning Hand, He gave me a deeper portion of Himself as I trusted Him in some really lonely seasons. I began to learn that God would give me all of Him that I made room for.

The pruning is what prepared the space.

The sovereign thing about the Lord, I'm learning, is that just when you think there couldn't possibly be any more left to prune in a certain area of bondage in your life, He sees more to prune. He searches the deepest depths. Only He knows fully the abundance that awaits.

For many years, I had led a Sunday School class to an amazing group of adults that I had come to know as family. The circle of people that I got to grow with during this season of teaching made an impressionable imprint on my life. I treasured and loved every aspect of leading Sunday school over the years.

One night, as I was on my way home from work, I felt the impression of God speaking over my heart and asking me to hand this ministry over. I wanted to unhear it, but I couldn't. I knew it was from Him, and yet, it felt crushing…shattering…devastating.

It felt like God was hurting me. It felt like He was taking from me. It felt like He was stripping so much away. Pruning feels like that. It hurts. It never feels good when something that's been a part of you for so long has been cut away.

I knew that the nature of God was not to harm me. I knew that, however, the cut was deep.

This prompting from the Lord was so clear, distinct and vivid that He literally told me the name of the very person that I was to hand this class over to, a man named CJ who had recently gotten saved, given his life passionately to the Lord and was leading his family in total surrender to the will of God for their lives. I knew that this prompting was from God.

We can trust the clipping of the Master's Hand if we know that every cut holds purpose.

Not every step of obedience is going to be an easy step. It can be the smallest act of faith to believe and trust in Him, and yet, it feels like the largest lunge sometimes. Walking in obedience in the midst of deep pain is rewarding, but it can still be very, very hard. Allowing Him to cut away at things and positions in our lives that have become more important than Him can be painful. Surrendering circumstances that have abused you and people who have hurt you can feel like everything inside of you is being ripped out from the inside.

It felt like He was ripping the only thing I had left in my grasp that I was using to search for identity in…and He was. That's exactly what He was doing. All this time, He was taking away every idol thing that I was using to find my worth and identity that wasn't Him. Every closed door was Him taking me deeper with Him. He was removing every single thing that I had begun to worship outside of Him. He was cutting away so that I could flourish. He was cutting away so that I could see Him. He was cutting away so that I could experience all that He had for me.

One thing I'm learning on this Jesus journey of pruning is this: *We can trust the clipping of the Master's hand if we know that every cut holds purpose.*

That very night, I went on a walk near sunset. In this season of my life where I felt very unseen, out of place, and set aside, not realizing that I was being set apart. I wept as I walked. I laid my heart out through tears. I listened. I wanted to hear what His heart was feeling, too.

I don't know everything about God, but I do know that His heart breaks when ours does. He doesn't neglect us in valley seasons. That's not who He is.

This clip from the Gardener's Hand hurt. It did. However, I knew He was taking care of me. I knew He was tending to the soil of my heart. In the midst of about 10 minutes, the sky lit up over me.

He brought me back to the story of Hagar in Genesis 16. Hagar's story is a powerful story of exodus. The term exodus literally means "the road out." It means a sudden departure or a way to escape. We can be like this. We can believe that the road out is by running from everything that hurts. We want to flee the minute life gets hard. This whole time, I thought the way of escape was in running from the pain that had been hurting me. I thought that if I could uproot myself from soil that felt undesirable, I could land my feet on new soil that might feel more comfortable.

Hagar's story is probably my favorite story in the Bible, and I think it's because it underscores how messy and complex God's work in our lives really is. This is a story of struggle and of how God meets us in the midst of what we are going through. God shows up in our stories in the messy parts. That is why I cling to Hagar's story so much, and it's why you should, too.

Hagar is introduced in the Bible as a slave woman who belonged to Abraham's wife, Sarah. Hagar wasn't elite. She didn't have an impressive resume. Since Sarah was unable to conceive, she gave Hagar to Abraham as a wife so that she might have children through Hagar. Sarah's impatience and yearning for a child are what pulled Hagar in.

Isn't it interesting how the impulsivity of wrong desires always leads to a rippling of the wrong things?

This decision would have long-lasting effects and consequences for Hagar. This is a good reminder for us that sometimes the pain in our lives is not a sole consequence of our own decisions. Sometimes the actions of others can have lasting effects on our lives if we allow them to. It doesn't mean that we shouldn't look inward and self-reflect on the areas where our tainted hands have polluted things and stunted our growth. It's simply the reality that there are festerings in our lives that we didn't welcome and we couldn't control.

After Hagar conceives, the dynamics between Sarah and Hagar drastically change. Bitterness and jealousy lead every decision moving forward. Pregnant Hagar, who is subject to Sarah's cruelty, runs away to the wilderness. She runs from humiliation and oppression.

I believe that the spirit of rejection was haunting Hagar in ways that aren't fully mentioned in this passage of the Bible.

Rejection is one of the enemy's favorite tactics and strategies in our lives. It keeps us insecure. It keeps us wrongly attached. It inhibits our ability to love people the way Jesus calls us to. It paralyzes us from operating in His will and way. Rejection makes us retreat. Not only did Hagar admit that she was running away, but she ran away into the wilderness. She didn't run towards God. She ran to the wilderness.

I think what I love most about God is that we can't outrun Him. The wilderness isn't out of bounds for God. In fact, the wilderness is one of the most frequently visited places that God chooses to encourage those whom He loves. Even when we run away, He is pursuing us. He did this for

Hagar, too. He pursued her and sent for an angel to meet her in her running. This Angel of the Lord meets Hagar in the wilderness and tells her to return and submit to Sarah. The Lord met her in the wilderness.

Moses used the following verse to remind the Israelites of how God protected them in their weakness.

> In a desert land, He found them, in a barren and howling waste. He shielded them and cared for them; He guarded them as the apple of His eye.
> Deuteronomy 32:10

It should comfort us to know that God can find us when we are lying in waste. No one else may even recognize that you are there. You may, like Hagar, be there all alone. You may feel like you have no one else who sees you in your hurt.

> The angel of the Lord found her by a spring of water in the wilderness, the spring on the way to Shur.
> Genesis 16:7

In our running, God is there. He pursues us when no one else does.

Your wilderness may have a different name than Hagar's. The wilderness that you are planted in will be different from mine. You probably are not beside the road to Shur. However, the landscape of your wilderness may be very similar. There are people who hurt us, betray us, and treat us unfairly.

You may be experiencing waves of rejection from someone who you pray would see your worth and value.

You may be struggling to forgive someone who has hurt you in ways that feel insurmountable.

You may be wondering how it is even possible to love someone who has betrayed you, where trust is very much broken.

You may be asking God how it is even possible to live amongst those who continue to treat you brutally.

You may be struggling, like Hagar, to even believe that God has a purpose for your life in this wilderness season.

God told Hagar to seek the welfare of those in her midst–to serve, to love, to submit, and to yield to His plan.

Friends, He is commanding us to do the same.

It's not really a suggestion. It's His command for us to experience the flourishing that He has for us. There are many days when it doesn't feel fair. There are days when it will be impossible if we are not attached to Him.

It is a daily surrender for me.

He may not release you from where He has you this season. We can run away completely, but it won't have been under His leadership or will for our lives. Hagar tried to run away, and God asked her to make a U-turn and return right back.

Our own life experiences can be complicated. We are human, and so are they. Sometimes it feels like there is more discord than healing. There is a lot of brokenness to live in and amongst . There will always be people in these spaces who do things under the name of Jesus that are the very opposite of the nature of Jesus. We have to acknowledge that we can be these people, too.

I came to a deep realization that if this is the soil God called me to, I have to stop opposing His plan for my life. God will not always call us to the soil we want. He will not always place us in nutrient-rich soil. Perhaps you are called to the soil you are, to enrich it, to seek the welfare of it. It provides an abundance of opportunities to love and show forgiveness and mercy.

I know the landscape that God is asking you to seek the welfare of looks different from Hagar's and even different from mine. That is true. The details may be different. The hurt you are experiencing may be different. The when and where and why, no doubt, are not the same. I know it feels like a wasteland. It feels like wasted soil.

Let me remind you: He has promises for each of us in this wilderness that we are in.

God brings assurance to Hagar and speaks His promises over her. He tells her that she will be the mother of a great nation! It is in this tender moment of pruning that Hagar is the first to name God: El Roi, the God who sees me. She was pulled in and then cast out. In that very moment, declaring these words, El Roi–the God who sees me, Hagar believed that God was looking after her.

> So she called upon the name of the Lord who spoke to her, "You are a God of seeing," she said, "Truly here I have seen who looks after me.
> Genesis 16:13

The God who sees.

And there she BORE her son Ishmael. Even in a place of unwanted ground, the Lord brought forth LIFE.

God laid His Word of truth upon my heart that evening as the sun set down upon me. I remember weeping through each step. My feet hit the blacktop of the pavement with rhythm while my heart clung to His promise over me:

And I declared His name…El Roi, the God who sees.

There are seasons where we all can feel like Hagar: pushed aside, cast out, in the wilderness, only to have God ask us to come back. It's hard to return to a painful place. It's hard to forgive when we keep remembering the pain. It's hard to submit in environments that are harsh.

Yet, promises are awaiting if we will surrender our lives to Him for His purposes. Even when we wander in wilderness places, even when life circumstances and systems of power push us down and toss us out, God is drawing near to us.

Be encouraged to look for God in the undesirable soil and to find assurance through your encounters with Him.

Hagar's story is a story of exile and a story of meeting God in the midst of pain and abandonment. Her experience of living in a foreign land was both agonizing and rewarding. Pregnant Hagar names her son, whom she has conceived for Sarah and Abraham, "Ishmael" which means, "God will hear". The son of Hagar, who was *just* a slave, serves as a reminder that God hears. He was attentive to this utterly marginalised and abused woman. And He is attentive to us. Even in our agony, even in our wilderness, He sees and He hears. God made Ishmael fruitful and multiplied him greatly. God promised Ishmael that he would be the father of 12 princes and raise up a great nation of His own! Would that have been so if Hagar didn't return with a heart to serve and forgive? I'm not sure. I do know, though, that God's promise for Hagar and Ishmael came to pass because she obeyed His instruction to return and seek their welfare.

Experiencing the blessings of all that God has for us is completely dependent upon our obedience in the wilderness seasons.

We may not be pregnant with an Ishmael, but we all are carrying a precious gift inside of us that the enemy wants to rob us of. The enemy wants to take what isn't rightfully his and wear us down by means of ridicule, abuse, and rejection. The enemy wants to make us believe that what we carry is not valuable, or that it doesn't belong to us. He sometimes can even use those in our midst, whom we would least expect, to trip us up. Abraham and Sarah should have known better. They knew God. They walked closely with God.

There was a season where I was navigating some really deep heart wounds. I found myself wanting to retreat like Hagar. I can vividly remember standing at church during worship in "my wilderness" and closing my eyes. Words that felt like they had been spoken to the Lord a thousand times came bubbling up yet again.

"God, I feel like I've been here a thousand times, but it doesn't <u>feel</u> any better. I keep bringing you the same things, but they don't seem to <u>look</u> any different. I'm still here in what feels like the wilderness. I'm still bitter. I don't know how to not be broken by it all. I am growing weary of trusting that you are using this. I need a resurrection of faith to believe that I'm not going to be overcome by this weight that is breaking me. Help my unbelief. I want to trust and believe that you see me here."

These are the words He etched over my wounded and broken heart:

> **"My attempt is not to change the landscape and scenery. My desire is to change YOU. If you give this to me, I'll begin to change your heart. If you would abide fully in me, everything that has the appearance of a wasteland won't look like that anymore. There's more for you than what you see right now. I can use you, if you'll let me. I have immeasurable fruit available for you through this pruning. You have been set apart UNTO Me. Stay attached to me in this season. Remain in Me and I will remain in you."**

You'll notice that His words back to me are in bold, and mine are not. That's intentional.

I was consumed with how I "felt" and only what I could see. If we sum up the quality of what God is doing in our midst based on how we feel and what we see, we will be in trouble! Our feelings will root us wrong. It will blind us to all that He is doing.

This conversation with the Lord was so pivotal for me. It became a marker for me that day. His words over me were louder than any lie that I'd been believing. I could feel Him driving down a spiritual trellis to help me abide. As He lifted me close to Him, I allowed the hot streams of tears to drip down over my cold heart.

Sometimes I need to focus on the battle that God wants to win in me more than the one I want Him to win for me.

What He did in that singular moment was enough manna for me for a lifetime.

After a few moments, the Lord prompted me to walk down to the center of the aisle during the prayer portion of the service. God was encountering me in the same way He came to Hagar. He found me in my distress and came to speak life, promise, and assurance over me. I truly believe that He needed me to believe His love for me. He desired for me to experience a tangible confirmation of all that He had in store for me that I was missing in my posture of wrong security and bitterness.

I stepped out in obedience. Sometimes the first step can be the hardest to take. I took the first step. I asked Him to show me what He wanted from me in this. This is a good reminder for each one of us: We don't have to see every step that He has for us just to take the first one.

I took the first step of what He had for me that day. I made my way down towards the center of the aisle where the altars were. Almost instantly, He showed me who I was supposed to pray over: the sweetest, young, blond-haired woman. I didn't know her very well, yet. Our paths had hardly crossed. I knelt down across from her on the altar, and God spoke over me:

"I want you to pray over this woman and bless her."

Can I tell you how intimidating that felt? It felt intimidating because I had spent a lifetime relying on myself. I had spent a lifetime striving to be used by God, to seek approval in so many forms. It was here that He just wanted me to abide in Him, to rely on only Him. To put my faith, hope, and trust in Him. To speak from His approval instead of for it.

I asked the Lord what He wanted me to pray over this woman, and He told me. He told me to pray about the calling that He had placed on her life. I prayed for her. I stood up when prayer time was over, and I found my seat in the second-to-back row again. Nothing felt remarkable. Nothing really felt any different. But I knew it was the step He was asking me to take—even when I could not see any others.

Even when it didn't really make sense.

Even when I was still in this place that I didn't want to be.

However, this time I knew it wasn't about me.

It was about Him.

I set everything aside that day and just clung to Him and allowed Him to lead me.

Here I was, being used by the Almighty God to pray for there to be revelation in someone else's calling—meanwhile, I'm still here in this Babylon season of my life.

A lot like Hagar, right? Receiving a promise from the Lord that she would be the mother of a great nation, meanwhile, He's asking her to return to everything that feels like lack.

It is imperative that we continue to hold fast to the promises that He speaks over our lives, most especially when we can't see any evidence of it. The Lord is good to those who wait for Him.

Refuse to rush His promises.

Over time, God brought an enrichment of soil through His revelation. There's not enough time or space to share the entirety of the whole story. However, in short, God used my obedience and willingness to be a confirmation for the sweet, young woman and her husband to enter into the ministry field.

Our giftings may not always seem significant. They may not initially seem impactful. They may not be front and center. But we are called to use the gifts we have for Him in ways that honor Him and build others up.

When God puts a gift in you, when God deposits something into your soil, when He has called you to make a difference for His name, He will begin to prune and prune and prune. Things may hurt you; things may break your heart, and you won't know why. You may not see the reason, and it won't feel good, but let Him prune. If you can push past the disappointment and press through the need to know it all, there will be an Ishmael gift in you. When your gift comes forth, God is going to do something exceedingly and abundantly above all you would ever ask or think or imagine.

Your calling and giftings may not be fully discovered yet. Your calling and giftings may not be all that desirable to you right now. You may wish you were gifted in different areas. You may be struggling to be used at all by God. I want you to know that it is okay to wrestle with the Lord. It is okay to share the deepest parts of your heart and hurts with Him.

He wants a relationship with you. It isn't perfection that He needs. He is concerned about who you are becoming–not all that you are doing. Our lives can be really messy– just like Hagar's was.

We need to talk about how messy the healing process with the Lord actually is. It can feel like a crushing season of allowing God to show you your unhealthy habits and sinful patterns.

Hagar wanted to stay bitter. God knew she would be poisoning herself and every offspring to come.

Healing is cooperating with Him to pull out every unhealthy root that is keeping you attached to the wrong vines. The pruning season will hurt. It will. The cuts will feel really deep. What's left of your frame may not feel all that impressive. There's going to be an appearance of lack. A lot will become exposed. Hold fast. There's an abundance of flourishing that is on the horizon. He can do more with your surrender than you can do with your control.

Even in the mess, even in all the rejection, even in the running, even in the wilderness, He wants to use you! This is good news for those of us, like Hagar, who are less than perfect. This is good news for those of us who are wandering in the desert places, who weep over the consequences of our own decisions, and those of us who have experienced abuse or rejection at the hands of others. It is among those that Jesus is to be found, ready to meet us at that place of despair. God comes to us in wilderness places.

Hagar was a slave whom He turned into the mother of a great nation! It was probably hard for her to believe that promise when she felt like she was just a slave, just a tomato plant. It was probably hard for her to believe that when she was planted in a place that felt painful. However, she trusted that God still saw her. She chose to meet God in this painful endurance and survive and adapt.

It was that day at church, that I, too, chose to meet God in this painful endurance and survive and adapt.

Trusting that He is…El Roi–the God who sees me.

As I stand in the midst of an agonizing wilderness, He brought me this clarity:

You are Chosen.
You are Loved.
You are Blessed.
You are Forgiven.
You are Important.
You are Free.
You are Victorious.
You are Valuable.
You are Gifted.
You are Saved.
You are Holy.
You are Redeemed.
You are Worthy.
You are Treasured.
You are Unique.
You are Enough.

REFLECT

- In Hagar's running, she encounters God and He calls her by name. Think of a time that felt like a wilderness time in your life? How did God show up for you? How did He meet you in that place? Take a few moments and journal about the wilderness that you are experiencing right now, even.
- How does declaring El Roi–the God who sees me, bring you comfort?
- God promised Hagar that she would be the mother of many nations. What promises do you hear the Spirit saying to you for you, your family, your church, your community?

SCRIPTURE

> So she called to the name of the Lord who spoke to her, "You are a God of seeing," for she said, "Truly here I have seen him who looks after me."
>
> Genesis 16:13

PRAYER

El Roi, nothing is hidden from You. You take my broken pieces and envelope them in Your tender care. You know my heart and understand everything about me. Truly Your eye is on me. I rely on Your unfailing love for me. My hope is in You. You are my help and my shield. I receive Your promises over my life. Amen.

CHAPTER FIFTEEN

New Skin

One of my very favorite weekends of the year is the weekend that Jeremy and I take off and drive an hour and a half north to do some Christmas shopping in early December. Often, the landscape is draped with a blanket of the most beautiful coating of white, winter snow. The air is brisk and cold, but we are together. Usually with a cup of sweetened, hot coffee in one hand, we link our free hands together and take off to deplete his work Christmas bonus.

It's our favorite time of the year!

This weekend, for us, brings relaxation, connection without the noise of the kids, and an opportunity to fill carts full of all the things that the kids have spent all year salivating over. After a full day of hitting our feet to the pavement, we usually go back to the hotel, change into something a little more elegant, and spend the evening debriefing the day at our traditional dinner spot: Johnny's on Fleur Drive. I spend all year waiting for this weekend. It beats any birthday or anniversary celebration because it's tradition and it's all ours.

This particular "Annual Christmas Shopping Getaway" (ACSG) threw us for a loop. We had just pulled into the very first store, and my phone started ringing. I pulled my phone out of my purse to read the screen: School Nurse.

"Oh no! I wonder if one of the kids got sick at school?"

I gestured to Jeremy that I was going to step outside the store so that I could take the call. What came next would change the next several months of our lives. I answered the phone and could immediately hear our 6-year-old daughter, Hattie Pearl, screaming at the top of her lungs in the background of the speaker. "Your daughter was at recess and asked if she could go inside to use the restroom. With all of her winter snow gear on, while attempting to open the recess doors that lead inside, her finger got trapped in the door. It is critically severed. She needs to get to the doctor immediately."

Here I am, wishing I could embrace her, so deeply wanting to be next to her in her pain. Yet, I couldn't. I was far from home at this point. I let Jeremy know what was going on. I knew how much this weekend meant to him, to both of us. Due to the fact that we were so far away, we made the decision to send his mom and sister to pick her up from school and keep us posted. That was not easy on my mama heart, but God provided His peace over me as He assured me that she was well taken care of. I knew this weekend provided an invaluable strengthening in our marriage.

We had no idea the months that were ahead. Not only did her finger need to be pieced back together, but her finger was also fractured from the blunt force of the door. Infection was also a huge concern. Following the direction of the surgeon's request, she was not allowed to return back to school until further notice.

One phone call can literally change your life.

I know you all can relate to that last sentence. You've been there, too, where your throat drops to the pit of your stomach and you are forced to process some really hard moments.

Almost immediately, Hattie Pearl got stitches in an attempt to attach the pieces of the finger back together. We spent the following weeks and months tending to the fractured pieces of this tiny, little middle finger.

Over time, these stitches had embedded themselves underneath layers of her skin. I could see what was happening every single time I changed the dressing on her finger. The stitches were embedding themselves underneath scabs. When the appointed time for the stitches to be removed came, not only did the stitches have to come out, but the scabs had to be peeled off first just to get to the stitches.

There are times in my own life when the very thing that needed to be removed had become buried underneath a mound of other layered pieces. The stitches were not bad. They served a purpose. That purpose was over. Stitches are only ever intended to be a temporary binding for what's broken.

The removal of things in our lives, no matter how freeing and healing, will often result in the reemergence of initial pain. It hurts to allow God to remove something, especially when what He needs to remove is buried underneath years of hardened skin. It is hard to part with something when the soil of our hearts has become so hard. No amount of striving will ever bring us to a place of complete healing.

Looking back over my life, I think the hardest thing for me to part with has been the idea of what I thought things would look like. Things often look different from how we envision them. Sometimes it's not the road we would have chosen or the paths we wanted to take. It can come with more heartache than we ever wanted woven into our stories. There are depths of devastation that we never saw coming and did not welcome.

There were seasons in our marriage when my husband and I let stitches stay way too long. We both were in so much pain with what we were enduring on our own that we were no longer attentive to the scabs that were growing over the stitches of one another's hearts and minds. When that happens, you no longer have to just remove the stitches, you have to remove the scabs that have also dried and formed over the pain and wounds, as you have put off true healing.

I was lying over Hattie Pearl's side as they were ripping open the scabs that brutally cold winter day, in order to expose the stitches. The weather conditions outside felt like mirroring the chill of everything we were about to face. I was literally lying on top of her in order to brace her body. All of her force was pushing back against me as she was trying to fight off the removal of these scabs. I knew the necessity of getting these hardened spots gone…I did. Allowing things to stay that do not belong anymore can create a festering of all the wrong things. It can cause infection in wounds that already exist. They needed to be cut out. I knew that it was what her finger needed to become what it could be. Watching her oppose the removal of these scabs felt like a parallel to all the years I spent fighting true healing.

As I embraced her, I whispered to her, "I know this hurts, but it's necessary. It has to be done. You're brave. This is what's going to make you stronger. Let them do this, even if it hurts. The pain won't last forever."

This is the voice of God over our lives as He prunes us.

At one moment, with tears in her eyes, she asked," Do they have to do this?"

In that moment, I got a tiny, microscopic glimpse into how God must've felt sending Jesus to us through the cross. In one climactic moment, filled with desperation and despair, Jesus asked His Father in the garden if there was any other way. Even Jesus asked for an alternate route. The very place where the mind of Jesus was tormented before His physical beating was called Gethsemane, the place of crushing. Oil and wine are both made through the crushing. We can't be all of who we are supposed to be in our calling if we do not see the value in the crushing. The crushing is what offers us His overflowing cup. Jesus knew He would face excruciating pain, pain that would ultimately lead to His death, but God knew it was necessary. He saw more. The crushing isn't the end. There's oil being made through the crushing.

There was a purpose for the pain.

There's a purpose for every pain we face, too.

His Word in 1 Peter 1:6-8 says:

> In all of this, greatly rejoice, though now for a little while you may have to suffer grief in all kinds of trials. These things have come so that the genuineness of your faith may be proven.

We need to live in the "SO THAT" piece of that scripture. There is a purpose for the pain. It is *so that* the genuineness of our faith may be proven.

God wants us to prove it, and sometimes the way out of it is the way through it.

Read that again!

Sometimes the way out of it is the way through it.

Suffering has the potential to make us holier, but only if we surrender to the process and allow God to do what He wants in us. This kind of refinement will not come when we live in opposition to God's methods. If we, like the Israelites, spend all of our time grumbling and cursing the soil around us, we will never experience all that He has for us through the pruning. We can't go around the method, the process, or the valleys to get to the promised land. The Israelites wanted the route to be shorter and with more ease. God knew better. The pruning fortifies us. It purifies us. It refines us. But we have to go through it.

The temporary pain does not compare to the soul work that God has breathed into us through it. The more I look back, the more I see that sorrow was my door to peace. Heartache led me to the gift I needed in Jesus. Sometimes we see it in fullness, but oftentimes, we see it in small threads that weave themselves together over time. After much time passes, we see a tapestry of beauty that only God could've seen first. If we have the ability to be aware, we will see that we have been changed by it all. That's a really beautiful thing.

About a month later, and after what felt like we had conquered the most devastating aspect of this finger journey, we were standing in front of what felt like yet another mountain.

I don't know about you, but I feel like mountains have this way of taunting us sometimes. They have this way of making us feel so small. Here we were, feeling like the size of an ant, staring up at Mount Everest again.

We met with the surgeon, yet again, who told us that there was a very good chance that our daughter would lose her finger completely, due to a lack of progression of healing. Even with having it sewn back together, patiently waiting, and then the painful process of removing the stitches, color pigmentation was not coming back into the tip of the finger. It did not appear that those severed pieces were going to have life in them again.

I have always loved the story of Ezekiel and the Valley of Dry Bones. Apart from their presence in a living body, bones are dead. Scripture says that these bones were dry. Not only were they dead, but they'd been dead a long time.

There are times in the wilderness season when that landscape feels like only that: dry, dead bones. Everything feels too far gone. We can be surrounded by everything that feels hopeless, by everything that feels beyond repair. The only thing that we could see was darkness up ahead.

Bones are what remain when life has passed. There may be bones everywhere in the valley you are in. Bones of numbness, helplessness, hopelessness, worry, sin, despair, grief, loss, sadness, depression, complacency, a lack of spiritual and emotional intimacy with God and others. When something has been dead for so long, we give up hope that it will ever live again.

God promises to fill these dry bones with life from His breath. He promises to bring flesh upon dead bones and cover them with new skin. God makes the once-dead and dry bones live.

How?

It is a work of revival, restoring life to something that once had life. This is not the creation of life from nothing. This is a resurrection, a restoration of life to something long dead.

Dead bones can never create life within themselves. We like to try, though, don't we? Even when we know that history has proven that, by our own means, our own striving, and through our hands, we are powerless to affect the resurrection that we know we desperately need, we still keep trying.

It is always God who resurrects.

It is always the breath of God spoken over us that affects change and brings life.

Never underestimate the power of a single Word from God. His Word always breathes life. Nothing is too far gone.

An appointment was made for the day after Christmas (which happened to be a Monday). At that appointment, the surgeon would, one more time undo the bandaging, and make a determining decision as to what the outcome would be.

There truly were just two options.

He would unwrap the bandages and find fleshy, pink skin, which would identify that life had started to come back into her limb, or he would open up the bandages, unwrap the wound and find grayish blue skin.

If that was the outcome, a surgery date would be set for amputation.

The day before this appointment, we were at church. It was a Christmas church service. I can remember the day so vividly. We were dressed in our Christmas dresses, and I was holding her clubbed hand. In the middle of singing "Joy to the World," my daughter looked up at me and asked, "Can we go down to the altar and pray?"

Now I don't know how many of you are familiar with altar time at your church services, but at our church we have altars that are set up near the front of the sanctuary. Typically, there is a prayer time portion during our church services where the pastor will open up the altars. During this time, you can come down and kneel at the altar and spend time talking to God: thanking Him, sharing burdens or griefs with Him, asking Him for discernment, wisdom, direction. It happens nearly every Sunday. Typically, people only go down to the altars during the prayer portion of the service.

This particular Sunday morning when my daughter asked if we could go pray over her finger, it was not prayer time. There was no one at the altars. We were in the second to last row in the back of the sanctuary. I wanted to honor her request, so I grabbed hold of her precious six year-old mangled hand and we headed down the long stretch to the wooden altars at the front of the church.

With every step, these words echoed in the backdrop: "Let every heart prepare Him room."

As we found our way to the altar and our knees hit the carpet, our hands linked together over that precious wooden altar, and I'll never forget her prayer: "God, will you save my finger so that I will always have 10 fingers to paint."

It may seem like a selfish prayer and maybe, in part, it may have been perceived as such, but she had been through the wringer. Her finger had been obliterated, she had endured some really painful nights of throbbing.

Even looking at it to clean the bandages of the wound had been really traumatizing for her.

What I heard was a six-year-old who was brave enough to prepare room in her heart for something of a miracle. I heard a six-year-old who was asking God not to let this storm go to waste. I heard a six-year-old who prayed with more faith and belief in God to resurrect dead things than I had.

In Ezekiel 37:3, God asks Ezekiel, *"Can these bones live?"*

God can resurrect anything that He wants to. Nothing is off-limits. He didn't need Ezekiel's partnership to revive the dead bones. However, God wanted Ezekiel to be a part of the resurrection. God doesn't need us, but He wants us to experience His resurrecting power in our lives.

Ezekiel had a part to play in reviving what seemed to be lost forever. We do, too.

I went to bed that night tense with anxiousness. I didn't want her faith to deflate over and over again as she would forever look upon an amputated limb. I just wanted God to come through for her. I knew He was able, but I didn't know if it was His will. The more that I learn about who God is, the less I want to pray outside of His will.

> For My thoughts are not your thoughts, neither are your ways my ways," declares the Lord. "As the heavens are higher than the earth, so are My ways higher than your ways and my thoughts higher than your thoughts.
> Isaiah: 55:8-9

His ways are higher than our ways, and I wanted the higher way for my daughter—even if it took longer, even if it didn't look like how I wanted it to look. I wanted the higher way.

Do we want that? Do we want the higher way of God even if it's more painful, even if it takes longer, even if the route is full of scenery we wouldn't choose?

Often, when my vision and thoughts are clouded with fear and doubt, I hear Him ask me to sing a song of praise instead. That's exactly what I began doing that night.

Isaiah 61:3 says:

> Grant those who mourn–give them beauty instead of ashes, the oil of joy instead of mourning, the garment of praise instead of a spirit of heaviness; that they may be called oaks of righteousness, the planting of the Lord, that He may be glorified.

When fear, doubt and uncertainty arise in our lives, He promises to give us beauty for ashes. He promises to give us joy in place of our mourning. He desires to clothe us in garments of praise so that the utterances of our lips can come against the oppression in our midst. Isaiah 61:3 is a promise we need to receive and a spiritual tool we need to learn to apply. It has the power to change not only our perspective but our very lives.

The next morning, we arrived at the surgeon's office. I hadn't seen her finger in a few days now (since we were supposed to try and keep it covered for 2-3 days at a time). They called her name, and we headed down the corridor to a small office with a little bed. She hopped up on that little bed and waited for the surgeon to come in and begin removing the dressing. As he peeled away layer after layer of banana yellow-colored gauze and dressing, he looked up at Jeremy and me and said, "Well, the skin is pink. I'm going to give it a few more weeks but I think she may get to keep this finger. And not only that, but after observing the results from her x-ray, the fracture that was once there has healed, too."

NO SURGERY NEEDED!

God had resurrected new life in her limb. What looked dead, now had life.

God has a way of doing that in our lives, doesn't He?!

He is continually taking the painful pieces, those things that look dead, and He is breathing new life into them.

He can turn dead ends into doorways!

When circumstances in our lives feel completely shattered to ashes, it's hard not to want God to hurry and fix it all. We don't want to have to step into the painful circumstances and seasons, but if we have to, we want the repair to be quick and fast and painless.

Suffering has the potential to make us holier, but only if we surrender to the process.

What if fixing and repairing isn't all that God has in mind for us in the shattering?

In my spiritual journey, there are days when God is pruning that feel really painful. They just do. I love you too much to tell you that it won't hurt. Every single time that God was cutting away the dead and overgrown areas in my life, it hurt. I didn't like it. There were many times when I told Him that I'd rather have the dead and overgrown if it meant not having to feel the cut. The pruning season can feel like you've encamped in the valley for a hundred years. It doesn't feel very admirable, and it sure doesn't look impressive. It's full of tenderness and exposure, whether you want it to or not.

The pruning season can feel shattering sometimes, too. When things are shattered to the point of devastation, it can feel a lot like dust–like ashes. We think that the shattering in our lives could not possibly be for any good. But what if the shattering is the only way to get ashes back to their basic form so something new can be made?

My spiritual growth is a journey.

Your spiritual growth is a journey, too. You'll never flourish if you don't allow Him to cut away at everything that doesn't look like Him. You'll never flourish if you don't choose to see value and worth in the shattering circumstances and painful places.

This pruning segment has taken me so long to write because I'm still in it. I'll forever be in it. It has given me a lot of time to process, reflect, and revisit. In many ways, it has felt like I have been asking God what He wants to show me in this valley season.

And yet, in the same breath, it feels like mountaintops of growth.

Of revelation…of visions…of soul work…of deep unraveling…of learning to trust Him—again.

With everything.

I began to know Him differently and more deeply.

Could God prohibit everything in our lives that doesn't feel good? Absolutely. He has the power and authority to do whatever He wants to. He's God. The problem with that scenario is that if He never allowed us to endure hardship, we'd never get to experience God as the One who resurrects dead things in our lives. We'd never get to experience Him as the redeemer of all that felt lost before. We'd never get to experience Him as the restorer of everything that was broken. There would be no beauty from ashes or joy instead of mourning. Beauty isn't fully appreciated unless you've experienced seasons of just ashes. His joy isn't fully comprehended if we've never felt Him mourn with us.

One evening, as I was undoing the dressing on Pearl's finger, it was the first time I looked at her finger and was amazed by the profundity of who God is and of what He is capable of. The first several weeks and even months were really hard to just look at her finger. I knew that the consistency of tending to the wound was necessary. However, it was hard to look at it and not be forced to look away. There was this one night where it all looked miraculously different, and I sat there amazed. It was the first time I could look at her finger, and my throat didn't hit the bottom level of my stomach.

I was holding her hand in the palm of mine and was peeling away outer layers of skin that were literally scaling off, layers of skin that were mashed by injury, by trauma, by pain. There was beautiful, new skin lying beneath the surface of that which was dying. That shattered dust residue in our lives, when placed in God's hands and mixed with His living water, can become clay. When you place clay into the Potter's hand, it can be made into something brand new. Ashes and dust don't signify the end. They are often what must be the first ingredient for the new to begin.

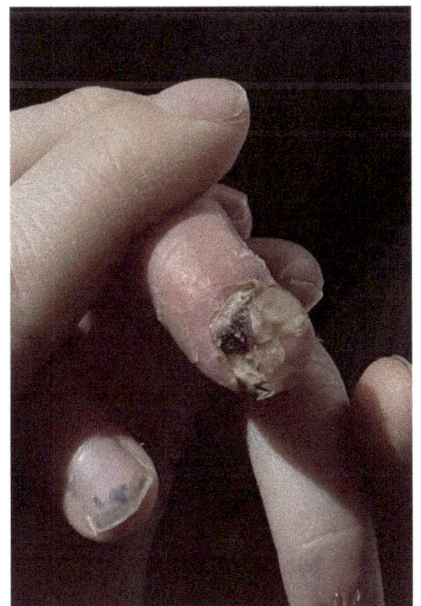

I wonder how many of us have been mashed by trauma, pain, heartache, disappointment, betrayal, rejection, or loneliness?

Even more, I wonder how many of us are moments away from new spiritual skin?

How many of us are moments away from a soul-cleansing healing that will allow all of the old to be peeled away to reveal and expose the newness of what God has been healing underneath.

Isn't it interesting that you don't get to gaze at the new until the old is gone?

Tending to the wound, whatever it may be, is necessary. What an honor to know that not only can God do the dressing and cleansing of our wounds, but that He wants to. Only God can breathe on that which was dead and resurrect it to new life.

Beauty CAN come from ashes.

Trauma doesn't have the last word.

The story isn't over.

He's doing something new!

The intricate and profound way that God heals is unfathomable.

It's unspeakable.

It's unimaginable.

It's beyond us. It should lead us to a posture of gratitude where all of our words fall short, realizing that all of this is much bigger than us.

REFLECT

- Stitches are only temporary. They may be initially necessary, but they aren't supposed to stay forever. In what ways do you feel stuck in your healing process? Have you grown comfortable in allowing your hurt to stay with you?
- When we stay stuck in opposition to the healing work God wants to do in us, spiritual scabs grow over the layers of things that were never meant to stay in our lives forever. Are you prepared to allow God to help you face these scabs and remove all that is unnecessary for your healing and flourishing?
- How can you live in the "SO THAT?" of 1 Peter 1:6-8. How can you offer a genuine faith to God in this season as you rejoice in all of it?

SCRIPTURE

> In all of this, greatly rejoice, though now for a little while you may have to suffer grief in all kinds of trials. These things have come so that the genuineness of your faith may be proven.
>
> 1 Peter 1:6-8

PRAYER

Lord, when you brought me to faith, what changed me was the grace that covered my sins and the mercy that promised me heaven. I sometimes wonder if I am supposed to experience fewer heartaches on earth since I am Your child. But then I am reminded that You use trials to refine my faith and to give me a deeper passion to long for heaven. Thank You for being not only the author of my faith but the finisher who makes my faith lack nothing in completeness. I claim the promise of Your Word over my life today from Isaiah 55: Your thoughts are not my thoughts. Neither are Your ways my ways. As the heavens are higher than the Earth, Your ways are higher than my ways, God. I want Your higher way over my shallow and limited way. Help me to press into Your will and Your way. I trust the process of what You know that I don't, and what You see that I cannot. In Jesus' name, amen.

CHAPTER SIXTEEN

He is in the Fire

I never thought I'd find You here

Sunrises and sunsets have always been my favorite things. There's just something that feels outside of this world that happens when you are blanketed under something that rises and falls the way the sun does.

I was on my way home from work one February night and was looking forward to getting the opportunity to watch the sun set yet again. My husband often jokes with me about my excitement over the sun setting,

"Babe, if you miss it, there will be another one tomorrow. It happens every night. They are all the same."

To me, they aren't. Each one feels so separate and distinct. The setting of the sun represents the capsule of another day, and there's profoundness in that.

As I found myself gazing into the night sky, this sunset definitely was different, one I had never seen before.

It was marvelous and strange. As I got closer to home and there was more visibility, I could tell exactly what was happening. The sun was setting down upon a field fire. Flames and smoke were engulfing the landscape, and the beauty of the sun was setting down upon it. You don't often see that happen at the exact same frame of time.

The two forces paired together were one of the most remarkable and profound things I've ever seen. The sky was screaming with smoke clouds, fiery and raging flames, darkness beginning to close in. In the middle of it all was the most magnificent and glorious sun setting upon it all. There was this light that pierced through it all. There was this splendor that, when paired with the fire, made it seem marvelous. What a beautiful thing to know that two contrasting things can cohabitate like that:

fire and beauty...

heartache and blessedness...

despair and hopefulness...

affliction and refinement...

sorrow and peace.

As I sit here, with hot tears beating down against a black keyboard, I am taken back to all the fires that I've found myself in over the years. There were moments in which the tragedy that I was living through felt too heavy to bear. There were moments when I wanted to give up. I can pretty confidently say that there were moments where I did. The soil of my field had undergone scorching heat. It had been choked out by every thorn imaginable. It had been sabotaged by the enemy, and I was left staring at the barren wasteland. There was a lot of devastation.

There were seasons where the smoke clouds rolled over, and my eyes lost sight of all that He was doing. There were seasons where the heat from the flames brought such pain that I wondered if He had left me.

I wondered if He forgot about me.

There were seasons where I questioned the process of what He was doing. The fire and smoke clouds can distort our vision.

Hebrews 12:29 describes God as a consuming fire. That can be a hard piece of scripture to delight in when you don't fully grasp it. Fire seems destructive in nature, and the results can appear completely devastating. A forest fire also seems intensely destructive because it appears that it consumes the entire forest, destroying property, damaging the environment and economy around it, and that's particularly why it feels so catastrophic. But a forest fire does not destroy forests — it revives them! Forest fires:

- Clean the forest floor of debris–opening it up to sunlight and *new growth.*
- Remove thick shrubs which take up the water, so the *water supply is restored.*
- Kills disease and insects which harm trees. The burnt vegetation *replenishes the soil with nutrients.*

Some species require the heat to open their cones and release their seeds.

Let that sink in!

Heat is often the agent used to bring about the abundance of what God has to release over our lives. Fire is so vital that forest managers use prescribed or controlled burning to reduce hazards and renew the forest.

"Change is important to a healthy forest," ecologists assure us. "Without fire, the trees and plants would eventually succumb to old age with no new generations to carry on their legacy."[1]

That's also true for us. Our legacy is preserved through fire: God's refining fire.

Who can endure it?

Who can stand through His fire?

I asked these questions to myself many times during the scorching heat seasons. Such questions imply trials, loss of privilege and possessions, perhaps even persecution. God's refining fire consumes the dead wood and thick underbrush…whatever is not authentic, what we coddle even if it blocks the light, prevents new growth, and consumes our resources.

Isaiah 48:10 became an anchor promise for me during the deepest pruning season of my life:

> Behold, I have refined you, but not as silver; I have tried you by the fire of affliction.

---

[1] Eaton, Diane. PresbyCan Daily Devotional; presbycan.ca

When we are being tried by fire and it feels like the heat is too much to bear, it may require us to go to the lowest places in our minds and invite Jesus to conquer those thoughts.

Do you need a weapon to kill the onslaught of the enemy over your mind? I have one for you:

> Though we live in this world, we do not wage war as the world does. The weapons we fight with are not weapons of this world. On the contrary, they have divine power to demolish strongholds. We demolish everything that sets itself up against the knowledge of God, and we take every thought captive to make it obey Christ.
> 2 Corinthians 10:3-5

The weapons that God gives us are weapons of Heaven. We have the authority to make every thought we have obey Christ.

Don't be afraid to go to the lowest places of your thoughts with Jesus. Going there alone may destroy you. Going there with Jesus will deliver you. We have to tear down every stronghold of every mental terror and ask Him to be *the* stronghold over our minds. The thoughts we have from the enemy don't have to be our stronghold because Jesus is our stronghold. He is our strong tower, our place of refuge, our fortress and safe place.

We have to stare at the "what if" questions and let Jesus command them to leave in His name. Here may be some of your "what if" questions:

What if this season never ends?

What if this pain never lets up?

What if these people never change?

What if you never remove me from this soil?

What if the conditions don't get better?

Is He still worthy? Is He?

What if your most frightening illusion becomes your reality? Is He still worthy? We have to answer that question. Daniel 3:17-18 says:

> Our God whom we serve is able to deliver us from the burning fiery furnace, and He will deliver us out of your hand. But if not, be it known to you, that we will not serve another or worship anything else.

We have to pre-decide that no matter what happens, we will not worship another!

God's refining fire may seem intensely destructive; little is left. It has taken me several years and a multitude of trials to truly understand and trust that the fires that God allows are never wildfires, but prescribed fires always under His control. His refining fire does not destroy us; rather, it refines and revives us, like a forest fire revives a forest. Out of the ashes arises new, healthy growth, and we begin to thrive again with vibrant faith, purified not as silver, but as gold.

There's a story in the Bible about three Hebrew children who were thrown into a fiery furnace because of their faithfulness to God. When the evil king came to witness their execution, he was stunned to see not three, but four men in the fire. He recognized that the fourth man in the fire was none other than the son of God!

The fires of our lives aren't to engulf us or even make us believe that all is wrong. These boys, Shadrach, Meshach, and Abednego, were thrown into the fire because of their faithfulness. We are never in the fires alone. The fires give us the opportunity to come face to face with our Immanuel, God with us.

Looking back now, I see so much of what He saw first. Never was there one fire that I was in alone. Never was there one that overtook me. They all brought refinement. They all changed me. Each one is a testament to the power and faithfulness of God over my life. Each one an opportunity to come face to face with my deliverer.

> This is what the Lord says: "Fear not, for I have redeemed you; I have called you by name, You are mine. When you walk through fire, you will not be burned; the flames will not set you ablaze. I am doing a NEW thing.
> Isaiah 43:1-2, 19

The fires of this life will come. They will. Hold on. God has His hand on the thermostat and promises that we won't be burned off. The nature of God is not to harm us and destroy us. The nature of God is to refine us.

You may find yourself engulfed in flames of fire today and suffocated by smoke clouds. You may not be able to see more than a few inches in front of your face. Let me speak His promises over you today:

- The flames in your life will sanctify you and draw you to Him in ways that nothing else can.
- It is in the furnace that offers the extravagance of beholding the beauty of the Lord as His presence rests upon you.
- While the furnace of affliction can be unspeakably hot, what we can gain through it is indescribably sweet.
- The furnace contains treasures that you won't find anywhere else.

Hard times can be the very soil that creates the holiest ground.

I was reading about the Judean desert one time. There's an acacia tree there in what is called the Holy Land. This particular tree is planted in a dry riverbed that rarely sees rain. Many pass by and wonder how it not

only lives there but thrives there. The answer? It has one of the deepest and most extraordinary root systems. Its roots reach deep into underground water sources.

The word "root" in Hebrew is "sheresh," which means permanence. That term is defined as: staying the same or continuing for a long time.

Like this acacia tree, we have the gift of finding life through hidden waters. He wants us to develop a root system that runs off in every direction towards His eternal stream. When our root system is consistently running towards His stream in every direction, no attack from the enemy will dismantle us. The enemy can come at us from any side, any direction and it won't shred us apart because we have deep roots that can withstand his onslaught.

Hard times can be the very soil that creates the holiest ground.

Our hardest and hottest seasons can become our most holy soil. It can be the exact environment designed for bearing the sweetest and most fruit. It's not about survival, or even endurance. It is a type of sacred reliance that leads to depths of transformation. There are times when we find ourselves in the desert seasons. In the desert seasons, comfort can feel distant, and challenges may continue to come.

Just as Jeremiah spoke to the Israelites in captivity, He speaks the same command and promise for us:

> Blessed is the one who trusts in the Lord, whose confidence is in Him. They will be like a tree planted by the water that sends out its roots by the stream. It does not fear when heat comes; its leaves are always green. It has no worry in a year of drought and never fails to bear fruit.
> Jeremiah 17:8

The promise is that in the hardest and hottest seasons…even then, most especially then…we don't have to be afraid. The heat will not kill us if our roots are in Him. What's more, we will bear fruit in this season that we may have never borne otherwise.

There is a purpose for every fire. There is a purpose in every "cut." There is a reliance that is born in the struggle. You are beginning to look so much like the Son who has *set* with you in every raging fire.

You're going to flourish. You will.

You're going to find, just as I did, watching the sun set that February night, that the cold does not last forever. The dark will turn to morning. The flames will let up. The smoke clouds will disappear.

You will be left with the greatest treasure of all: a deeper portion of Jesus Christ. He promises to turn our pain into purified gold that will last throughout eternity. Even amid pain, struggles, tragedy, tribulation, in the heat of the furnace, I feel His presence setting around me.

You aren't alone in the fire.

He is in the fire, too.

You are going to find Him in a place you never thought He'd be.

REFLECT

- As I watched the sun set down upon the smoke clouds of the field fire, it was marvelous and strange. How do you feel two remarkable forces cohabitating in your life right now (fire and beauty, heartache and blessedness, despair and hopelessness, affliction and refinement, sorrow and peace)?
- How does it comfort you knowing that God's consuming fire is not hazardous with attempts to destroy us, but rather, prescribed to refine and purify us?
- In this season, you may not be able to see more than a few inches in front of your face. Do you see value in fully relying on Him to lead you?

Ask God to reveal His purpose for these fires in your life. Begin to journal down what you hear Him revealing to you.

SCRIPTURE

> You let men ride over our heads; we went through fire and through water; yet you have brought us out to a place of abundance.
>
> Psalm 66:12

PRAYER

Lord, thank you for the promises that we can find in Your Word. I pray that my fire season is purposeful. I know that You are in it with me. Use my fire season to prepare me for the journey that You have ordained. No matter the fire, I will never be alone, and I will never be the same. Thank You for taking the time to prepare me for who You have called me to be. I pray that I never underestimate the value of this fire season. Amen.

CHAPTER SEVENTEEN

Remnants From the Ruins

The word "remnant" refers to the remaining quantity of something that is left over after an event or a catastrophe. It is what is reserved. There is always a faithful remnant left during times of hardship, persecution, and painful catastrophes in our lives. There is always a remnant that is left if we have the eyes to see it and believe.

It all holds purpose. Nothing is wasted.

Sometimes it feels like the war that is happening around and within us is tearing us apart. Battle wounds are being exposed. It feels like we are surrounded by only ashes, by everything that has been burned. Let me remind you that the fires of our lives hold incredible value.

A remnant may not be a lot, but it is enough. When you are in a spiritually dark season, it's not the end. It's hard to see what He's doing or where it's all going to lead. Believing gets hard when it looks as though there is no way out and no way through. We can't see what could be. We only see what is.

As I've looked back on all the ruins, I have seen His hand on every piece of it in my life. Even the rubble. He was my portion when nothing else was enough. Throughout every crumbling, He knew where every piece belonged.

It may all look like just a bunch of rubble to you right now, but they are going to be the remnants that He uses to breathe life into you and rebuild you.

There is always something left that proves that the hand of God was upon it. *Our lives are a remnant story.*

Do not discredit yourself if you feel as though you are limping. Do you remember Jacob from the beginning of the book, who laid His head upon a hard rock? Jacob wrestled with God and won, yet still limped through life. You have everything you need to be blessed, even if you have to crawl half the way.

I was doing dishes one morning and was gazing out my kitchen window. My eyes captured the landscape of my backyard, where my garden is planted. What I saw was shocking and magnificent. I saw the remains of last year's produce sprouting up. The Lord instantly spoke over me at that moment. A word from the Lord can carry us. And it carried me that day and in the seasons to follow.

Fruit is sprouting from the seasons passed.

I didn't experience the fruit last season. I saw it this season. There are seasons that we undergo that feel catastrophic. They feel earth-shattering. They feel wasted, but I was reminded, in this, that he wastes nothing. No circumstance, trial, or season is wasted under His umbrella of will and purpose.

Sometimes what feels like a delay isn't a delay at all. It's the remnants.

There are seasons when the weight seems too much to bear. There will be seasons where it feels like the heat will kill us. There will be seasons when we wish things looked different. There will be seasons when the cries of our hearts are desperate pleas.

It is in those seasons that God is planting seeds and watering.

It is in those seasons that God is doing His most precious refining work.

It is in those seasons that we are being rebuilt.

Trust that He isn't leaving your side. Trust that He is a good God with a good plan. Perhaps there's a flourishing that must first begin in the valley.

When we trust that there will be a remnant from the ruins, it changes everything. His word in Psalm 147:2-3 promises a rebuilding:

> The Lord builds up Jerusalem and brings the exiles back to Israel. He heals the brokenhearted and bandages up their wounds.

He is rebuilding our souls. When the Holy Spirit of God tears something down, it will be rebuilt with greater purpose and promise. We will weep at the sight of a new foundation. He is rebuilding every broken piece. He is restoring all that was ripped apart from the ruins. There are no damaged pieces that He can't make whole. He is redeeming all that was stolen. He is returning all the years that felt like they'd been taken. His goodness and mercy are washing over all the pain of your past. He is raising beauty from the ashes. What we see as broken, God sees as beautiful. His promise says:

> He will rebuild the old ruins and restore the places destroyed long ago.
> Isaiah 61:4

It's imperative that we don't lose sight of this promise. He will take the wreckage, all the rubble, and rebuild us. It may be through His consuming fire, but that's where the ashes are that He uses.

Do you remember the people of Israel that God sent to live in captivity for 70 years? Settling in soil that felt so undesirable for 70 years can feel tragic. One singular chapter after the prophet Jeremiah tells them to settle in exile, he also shares this promise from the Lord to them:

> I will restore the fortunes of Jacob's tents and have compassion on his dwellings; the city will be rebuilt on her ruins, and the palace will stand in its proper place. From them will come songs of thanksgiving and the sound of rejoicing.
> Jeremiah 30:18-19

the very same God who placed us in undesirable soil is the same God who becomes our source of nourishment to grow and flourish there.

The very same God that placed them into undesirable soil is the same God who became their source of nourishment to grow and flourish there. The same God who asked you to stay when it felt unfair and unjust, is the same God who hasn't forgotten all that you've been through for Him. The same God who sat with you in the fire is the same God who is refining you by it. The same God who allowed the ruins is the same God who will use the ruins to rebuild you.

Sometimes the ruins are so devastating that it feels as though God is destroying us completely. That is not so. Sometimes God does cut away at those things that aren't of Him, and sometimes God sends us into the fire for refinement, but we are not destroyed completely. Something will always remain. The seed, the remnant, will always remain.

If your ruins have stripped you of everything, there will still be a seed that remains. Although the seed will have seasons where it is buried, imprisoned in the dark earth, feeling lonely and empty, it will die to itself. It will be buried in the soil of repentance. It will receive nourishment from the sunlight of God's glory. It will be watered with His living water. Is the seed thriving or dying? It will be developing roots to be a tree! That's what it will be!

The ruinous experiences will always be painful. However, the ruins are not you. The ruins are just the ruins. They are for you to learn in, not for you to live in. You are being rebuilt upon them!

For ages, in the East, it was customary to build cities upon the ruins of places that had been destroyed in order to strengthen fortifications. The very foundation for the rebuilding is upon the ruins! The ruins aren't for nothing. They hold purpose. They are the very thing that, when we allow God to rebuild us upon, becomes the agent to strengthen the new. The ruins are there to be the infrastructure for your future flourishing and growth. They are your roots! They are your foundation. The ruins are now the reinforcement agent! No one else may see it, but the builder knows it's there. No one else may see it, but the Gardener knows that the remnants are there. That's where He chooses to rebuild–upon the ruins.

Our greatest disappointments, the things that shake us, break us, and make us question everything don't have to mean all hope is lost. We can place our lives fully in the hands of the Master Gardener, the rebuilder of our souls. We can stare at the undesirable soil, accept the clipping of His Hand, and trust that the Master Gardener is bringing about a harvest in our lives and in our fields that we can't even begin to imagine. We can dare to believe He is making something glorious out of dust–out of us. We can dare to believe that there will be remnants from the ruins. It's what is left in us after a harsh season of what looked like and felt like a catastrophe. There are remnants of goodness all over our lives. Every season we walk out of has the ability to give evidence of His work in us.

Every time you trusted Him when you wanted to run from Him, roots went down!

Every time you opened your Bible when you felt unseen, roots went down in Him!

Every time you worshipped when you didn't feel it, roots went down!

Everything we were is buried underneath everything that we now are!

I was walking near a downtown square one day and saw a beautiful building being torn down. It wasn't just any building. It was the building where my husband had bought a promise ring for me nearly 20 years prior. Clearly, they had been tearing it down for several days because by the time

I caught a glimpse of it, all that was left were the ruins of piled bricks.

There was a group of people standing on the sidewalk watching this building being torn down.

I started up a conversation with a lady who was standing near me, and I said, "This is sad. The building was beautiful. It's hard to see it go, isn't it?"

She looked at me with a smile on her face and said, "The building belongs to me. It looked beautiful on the outside, but its walls were caving in. Structurally, it was facing collapse at any point. It had to be torn down. Don't worry. We are planning a rebuild."

If you look at the corner of this building, you will see the walls actually bending into collapse. The owner of this building told me that that literally happened in a matter of a few days. No one could even tell prior that anything was even wrong.

I asked her how it happened so quickly.

She said to me, "I was told that didn't happen overnight. The collapse was a culmination of everything that had happened over years that no one could even see."

Friends, there may be a culmination of collapse that takes years in the making to finally break.

That is my story.

Only the builder can see the collapse that is coming. Only God knows that the ruins won't be wasted. Repair isn't always sufficient enough. Sometimes there has to be a complete demolishment in order to rebuild with strength and fortification.

God will not tear something down or allow something to collapse that He does not intend to rebuild with greater purpose. He isn't concerned about keeping the beauty of the building if it is facing an inward collapse.

Just like those standing on the sidewalk watching the tearing down of this old building, there will be a gathering of people who are watching what it looks like to be torn down. The rebuilds are more exciting and sometimes more impressive. There is always a gathering of people who will watch that. But there is also a gathering of people who want to watch what it looks like for every stone to be removed.

The remnants of the ruins are a place of testimony, if we allow it to be.

As I started to walk away from the rubble, my eyes caught black wording on the window next to the building that was being torn down. It said: "Perhaps this is the moment for which you have been created."

The rubble doesn't define us. But the rubble can be the very pieces that are used to refine us. The rubble can be the very grounds where our testimony is. The rubble can be the soil where we've fully surrendered.

We are going to be able to see it all more clearly once the rebuilding begins. The silence that once felt so useless has now found its purpose. The rubble wasn't wasted; it was worth it. The wait that felt like it was going to kill us offered us a rebuild. We are stronger now! We are rebuilt with an even greater appreciation of our builder.

May the declaration of our lips be that He never left us and He's never failed us.

He's the God who came through every single time, on time.

May a remnant always be a rebuilt life that looks more like Jesus.

REFLECT

- As you look back over some of the most painful and catastrophic seasons in your life, what were the remnants that God left? What of value was left after your valley season?
- What fruit do you see in yourself from a season past?
- How do you feel God rebuilding you upon the ruins? Write down some identifiable ways that you notice Him rebuilding you.

SCRIPTURE

> This land that was laid waste has become like the garden of Eden: the cities that were lying in ruins, desolate and destroyed, are now fortified and inhabited. They will know that I, the Lord, have rebuilt what was destroyed and have replanted what was desolate. The Lord has spoken, and I will do it.
>
> Ezekiel 36: 35-36

PRAYER

Lord, thank You for rebuilding from the rubble for my good and Your glory. Thank You that no circumstance is too far gone for You to bring about healing. Thank You that You aren't afraid of my brokenness. You are the great architect, our Creator, the One who knit us together in our mother's womb. You know the scars, the wounds, and every circumstance that I have been through. What I see as broken, You see as beautiful. You know where each piece belongs. When I put my trust and hope in You, piece by piece, You are putting me back together into something more beautiful than before. You are the God who promises to rebuild from the rubble. I have something to sing about. Amen.

I beg you to change the landscape.
Please alter this scenery.
But You bring the constant reminder
The thing You want to change is me.

A sacred scalpel in your hand
I want to trust what you'll do.
So cut it all away
Until all that's left is you.

In the midst of the breaking,
When it feels like I won't survive
He can do His deepest work in me,
Preparing me to thrive.

Who I am becoming
Is at the very core.
And pruning is what prepares the space
For me to know You more.

What if the only way out,
Is to walk right through this fire?
Instead of fleeing from refinement,
And dragging branches through the mire?

Every cut holds a purpose,
When in you I will abide.
You will rebuild these ruins
When I'm wholly purified.

PART FOUR

Flourishing

To grow or develop in a healthy or vigorous way, especially as the result of a particularly favorable environment.

CHAPTER EIGHTEEN
The Proof is in the Fruit

This flourishing segment is a really hard one for me to write, all while feeling a sense of completion. There are still a lot of aspects in my Jesus journey that I fall short in. There are areas that I am still surrendering to Him. There are still areas that need to be pruned. The process to a flourishing and sanctified walk with the Lord is just that, a process. To say that we have arrived is a lie to ourselves. Arrival speaks of destination.

Friends, we will never be flawless on this side of Heaven.

There will never be a time when we have "arrived." We are continually learning how to attach ourselves to Him in the here and now. We don't need another destination. We need an invitation. An invitation from the Heavenly Father to continue to sift and sanctify us.

We need His presence.

When I began writing this portion, I asked Him for his guidance and direction. I asked Him to show me the areas that I need to look more like Him and less like me. This flourishing segment is not a complete depiction of everything that I have figured out, but rather, all the ways that I'm still pursuing Him and relying on Him to sustain me.

When I look back on what God has done through every pain and every path, the opportunity and boldness He has equipped me with to not only overcome the hurt that I have faced, but also to be an encouraging force for others as they realize all they have left is all that they need, feels really humbling.

John Chapter 15 has become my life passage. I personally do not feel that there is any section of the Bible that has impacted me, inspired me, sharpened me, held me, and given life to me more than this one.

> By this, my Father is glorified that you bear much fruit,
> and so prove to be my disciple.
> John 15:8

The calling of our lives is not about us. If it ever becomes as such, we have missed the greatest prize that has ever been given to us. Any increase, favor, or influence in our lives is for the glory of God and Him only. God's desire is for us to be fruitful. His desire for our lives is an abundance of love, joy, peace, patience, kindness, goodness, faithfulness, gentleness, and self-control. He tells us in His Word that He is glorified when we bear fruit. He tells us in His Word that it is the very proof of whether we are His disciples or not.

Do you know that old saying, "the proof is in the pudding?" It means that the value, quality, or truth of something must be judged based on direct experience with it. The proof of how good the pudding is can be found in the eating.

Do you want to know how well someone is abiding? Look at how much fruit they have.

Do you want to know how much time someone is spending with Jesus? Look at how much fruit they have.

Do you want to know how much someone loves Jesus? Look at how much fruit they have.

In this case, the proof is in the fruit.

As we've seen in Jeremiah 17:7-8:

> It (the plant/tree) does not fear when heat comes; its
> leaves are always green. It has no worries in a year of
> drought and never fails to bear fruit.

The beautiful flourishing of the Lord is not limited by our circumstances. It isn't limited by what's happening around us. It isn't limited by our pain, our disappointments, our wounds, or even our lack of understanding. When we stay close to Him and are connected to the vine, we can undergo immense heat through painful circumstances and still bear much fruit for Him. In fact, we are called to bear fruit for Him in every season of our lives.

One thing I am learning in this flourishing season is this: I'd rather have the fruit of the Spirit than the gifts of the Spirit. Are gifts thrilling? Absolutely. Do they serve an earthly and heavenly purpose? They sure do. He promises to give us gifts from His Spirit. His gifts are given. The fruit of the Spirit, though, is *grown*. The gifts are His power in us. The fruit is His character in us. His Word says that people will recognize that we are His by our fruit, not our gifts. This type of character is forged and rooted in our daily decisions to honor God even when no one is watching.

I'm thankful for the gifts He gives. However, we shouldn't care how well we can pray if we aren't kind. We shouldn't care how much talent we have if we aren't loving. We shouldn't feel impressed with how significant our titles are if we are not faithful in stewarding them. We can be prophetic, but who wants to listen to what we are saying if we don't have joy? We can draw a big crowd, but if we aren't even ministering inside our own homes, what's it all for? The fruit that we bear always reveals the root. Good fruit will always start at the root. In John 15 v.15-16, Jesus says:

> I am the vine, you are the branches. I appointed you to go and produce lasting fruit.

To produce the kind of good fruit that leaves a great taste in the mouths of those we encounter, we must have a healthy spiritual life. That means that we prepare the soil where He has planted us. It requires that we grow by being rooted in Him. It requires being regularly fertilized and fed through our daily time in His Word through prayer and worship. We have to be nourished to flourish!

A frightening thought for some of us is that it also requires that we allow the Master Gardener to prune us with His careful shears. In trying times here and now, and in the ones to come, we must remember who we belong to! *The fruit always reveals the root.*

*the branch that
bears the most fruit
is the one that bows
the lowest.*

When we prepare the soil, are well-watered, well-fertilized and well-pruned, our roots will be strong, and we will yield lasting fruit. Our spiritual trees will be dangling with fruit that we never thought imaginable. Friends, the fruit that we bear in the flourishing isn't so that we can boast in our abundance. No! It's so much bigger than us. The fruit that we bear in the flourishing is so that we can bless through our abundance.

You'll know when you begin to flourish because the people in your midst will become more precious than any position.

My mom shared a picture with me of a fruit tree out in her yard loaded with fruit. There was so much fruit on the tree that the limbs were nearly touching the ground! It was a sight to behold.

Do you know what it made me think? The branch that bears the most fruit is the one that bows the lowest.

The one who flourishes lives out the call of Jesus in Matthew 20:28:

> Just as Jesus did not come to be served, but to serve, and
> to give His life as a ransom for many.

The one who flourishes is the one who is fully abiding and relying on Him. It's the tree that doesn't need honor or praise. It's the one that has roots deeper than will ever be seen or known. The flourishing one is the one that seeks no personal gain. There's no motive or secret catch with the flourishing one. The flourishing one is the one whose roots go down deep, and the result is an abundance of lasting fruit that's all about Him. The fruit that the flourishing one bears is for the blessing of whoever and whatever purpose God has for it. Its humble and hunched posture is not a sign of weakness but a display of God's faithful flourishing.

REFLECT

- How does it make you feel to know that God chose you to be a bearer of every good fruit?
- There's a richness to being joined with Jesus. He sources us to bear fruit that we've never known. How do you see evidence of this in your life right now?
- If you were to be a fruit inspector of your own life, what fruit do you see the most of? Which fruit do you see the least of?
- What value do you find in living a life of service?

SCRIPTURE

> You did not choose me, but I chose you and appointed you that you should go and bear fruit and that your fruit should abide, so that whatever you ask the Father in My name, He may give it to you.
>
> John 15:16

PRAYER

Heavenly Father, thank You for the depth of truth that is to be found in Christ, my true Vine. Thank You for choosing me to be a living branch on Your Vine. I thank You for the pruning seasons where You take away all in my life that is not fruitful. Through You, may my life bear fruit abundantly. Help me to grow in grace and live and work to glorify You, as I abide. In Jesus' name, amen.

CHAPTER NINETEEN
Take Me There

Being a parent teaches me so much about what my walk with the Lord should look like. When my daughter was a toddler, she spent several years being persistent about not going anywhere without me. Nearly every time I would ask her to do something, she would respond, "Take me there." If I'm being utterly honest, there were days when I just wanted her to go by herself. When I would encourage her to go on her own, she would reply, "Not alone, Momma."

There is this profound reliance that Moses in the Bible gleans from his changed root system. In Exodus 33, Moses speaks to the Lord and says,

> If Your Presence does not go with us,
> do not send us up from here.

Moses knew the necessity of being in the presence of God. His calling may have begun when he was full of insecurities and doubts, but it evolved and grew into this incredible picture of him being a reliable vessel to be used by God. He grew deeper roots, and his heart became more reverent. He knew that he didn't want to take a step without God any longer.

During this season of motherhood with my daughter, I often prayed for a renewed spirit and a fresh joy. There were days when I grew weary of having a constant shadow of someone needing me for all things. There was a restlessness in having someone clinging to me for every single step.

While there were days when I felt worn out from walking everywhere with my daughter, that's not the nature of God. He doesn't grow weary of us. His heart's desire is for constant fellowship with His children.

In the very beginning of creation, in Genesis 3, God provides a beautiful picture of His intentional design. Constant communion with His creation is the rhythm of the heartbeat of God. From the beginning of time with Adam and Eve in the garden, his deepest desire has always been to walk closely with us.

We need Him. He wants us.

One particular day, it felt as though God paused time and fixed my gaze on something so significant and special. In an instant, my daughter's request, "take me there," allowed me to see the beautiful picture that God wanted me to see. Sometimes I miss it. I'm forever grateful that I didn't miss that particular day. That day, I watched my daughter be secure in her steps only because of the hand that held hers.

I knew instantly that I'm the same way. He desires to "take us there."

One of my favorite hymns, "I Can't Even Walk" was written in 1974 by a man named Colbert Croft. My favorite part of the song says:

> *I think I'll make Jesus my all in all.*
> *And if I'm in trouble on His name I'll call.*
> *If I didn't trust Him, I'd be less of a man.*
> *'Cause Lord, I can't even walk without You holding my hand.*
> *I can't even walk without you holding my hand.*
> *The mountains are too high and the valley is too wide.*
> *Down on my knees, that's where I learned to stand.*
> *'Cause Lord, I can't even walk without You holding my hand.*

We all have significant moments where God meets us in our midst and leaves us in wonder and awe. There was a significant moment, in the very center of the Babylon season of my life, where I made a declaration with my heart and lips. That declaration gave me the fervor I needed to keep pressing in, to keep trusting, to keep surrendering my will to Him, and to keep pursuing Him above everything else.

Above every hurt.
Above every lie.
Above every heartache.
Above every feeling of loneliness.
Above every wrong desire.
Above the tangled knots in my heart.
Above all of it.
The declaration was this:

> I can do anything You ask me to do, Lord. I can stay anywhere you ask me to stay. I can serve anyone you ask me to serve. I can love anyone you ask me to love. I will go wherever you ask me to go. As long as You are the One who will "take me there."

While declarations are important and powerful, sometimes God asks even more from us. There are times when God asks us to do things that are outside of our comfort zone in order to test the genuineness of what we declare. Sometimes we have to stand in front of painful places to truly heal.

Sometimes the way out of it is the way through it.

There's a story in the Bible about a man named Joshua who was appointed by God to lead the Israelites into the Promised Land. This story is a powerful account that demonstrates the faithfulness and might of God. It is part of the fulfillment of the greater promise that God made to the Israelites that they indeed would enter the Promised Land.

In this story, Joshua led the Israelites to a city named Jericho. This city was surrounded by walls so high that no one could get in. It was their form of protection so that they would not be overthrown. God gave Joshua very specific instructions on what to do to cause the walls of Jericho to collapse so that they could defeat Jericho and claim the city that He had for them. Their instructions included carrying the ark (God's presence at that time) and marching around the city walls while declaring praise! To many, this may seem absurd and outlandish! This is not the typical method many of us would choose to overthrow a city. However, Joshua obeyed the promptings of the Lord, and after seven days, the walls fell down.

On a cold day in January, I had just sat down in front of my laptop to begin writing this flourishing segment. I had my favorite pen in my hand, my caramel coffee lingering to my right, and my favorite Hosanna Bible open to my left. My mind was creatively overflowing with all that God may have me write. In an instant, the Lord pricked my heart. I could literally feel Him pivoting me. I have not always liked to pivot in my spiritual walk, but I am beginning to learn that the pivots are small, acts of obedience that bear more fruit.

Friends, we can be saved, love Him with our whole heart, and still need deliverance in areas of our lives.

Just like Joshua, He gave me instructions towards a long-awaited victory that day. He led me to a place that He had prepared for me to conquer, and He asked me to circle it with Him and worship Him until He said we were done. That was His only instruction: carry His presence, circle what needs torn down, and declare praise. Sounds pretty identical to the instructions He gave to Joshua and the Israelites for their victory into the Promised Land.

If we want to enter into all that He has promised for us, we have to be willing to do exactly what He asks.

We might not understand every instruction.

I didn't.

I didn't know what it meant.

I didn't understand it.

In an act of obedience, I set my Bible and assignment aside. It no longer seemed like the most important thing. *We can love His Word and not live His Word.* That makes us hypocrites and cowards. *We can be more infatuated with Him using us than Him changing us.* I had lived that long enough. It was no longer fulfilling.

I laced up my black Nike tennis shoes, threw on a hat and gloves, stepped off my front step, and into the blistering 11-degree blasting winds. I started running towards what He had for me. I began circling the space with Him.

Flourishing looks different for each one of us. It really does. The outcomes of what we want are not instant, and our "flourishing" often looks different from what we initially thought it would. The Israelites were not permitted by God to simply storm the city when they wanted to. How much easier would it have seemed for Joshua to instruct the army of 600,000 Israelites to siege it instead? It probably would not have taken seven days. However, God asked the Israelites to wait, pray, and praise. They had to listen closely to God's instructions and follow. They marched, they camped, they waited on God to move.

Without the power of God, the Israelites could have marched around those walls a million times, and nothing would've changed. They could have blown a thousand horns and shouted until they lost their voices, but without God's authority, the walls would have never fallen. We truly need God. We need God to win our battles, to deliver us from things holding us back, to empower us to love others, to overcome the obstacles in our way, to seek the welfare of the places where He has us, in the soil right where we are.

My feet hit the pavement, the wind beat abusively against my face, and the presence of the Lord rested on my heart and mind. Even when the circumstances in your life feel abusive, God is resting over your heart and mind. Greater is He who lives inside of us than anything in this world. God's power living in us is stronger than anything we will ever face.

The gravel underneath each step felt as shifty as everything I had given my life to before Him. He showed me so much as I circled with Him that day. Sometimes, the aftermath of really deep pain creates some really high walls. We have built walls so high that no one can get in. It becomes our form of protection. God is willing to crawl over walls to be with us. Nothing stands in the way of His pursuit. But He's also the God who wants to tear them down completely so that we can see the depths and lengths of His love.

God told the Israelites to carry His presence, to circle and march around walls that needed to fall for their victory. He told them to pray and praise. Aren't you thankful that we serve a God who isn't afraid to tear down some really high walls so that we can experience the land that He has promised for us? We must be willing to identify the walls that need to be torn down in our own lives. We must be willing to pray and praise as we wait for victory.

I am finding that the method to victory isn't always the quickest measure. God is not a genie to be used. He is a God to be experienced and known.

That day in January was a day of victory and healing for me. Initially, writing felt like the more pressing need that day. It felt like the task and assignment that would leave me more accomplished. However, if the Israelites had resisted the instructions God gave Joshua, the walls of Jericho would never have come down. Their obedience to God allowed them to enter the promised land and flourish. My obedience to praise Him, even in places that are some days still tender, is what makes the stone walls begin to crumble.

God's presence never left my side that day. I could feel Him saying:

> **"I'm going to circle this space with you, and you are going to seek its welfare. Do you not remember my command for you in Jeremiah 29:7? Seek the welfare, and pray on its behalf, for in its welfare, you will find welfare. If it prospers, you will also prosper. If it flourishes, you too will flourish."**

Our feet are entering the promised land, one crumble of a stone at a time, when we live out this command in Jeremiah. I am not a runner, but that day I ran for nearly two hours. I wept the entire time.

Seeking the welfare of undesirable soil may look like this:
Blessing those who have hurt you.
Praying for those who have mistreated you.
Serving those who have stolen from you.
Asking God to allow people and places in your midst to prosper.
Realizing that if the soil you are in flourishes, you will also flourish.
If we flourish, those in our midst will flourish, too.

I may not have been holding a trumpet, but I may as well have been. It was my song of triumph and praise. No matter what we face, or however long it takes, there is a victory on the way. What once felt like rubble and ruin, now felt like a freedom parade.

God will prove that
He can be found in
soil just like this.

I didn't invite my entire prayer team of mentors and closest friends to circle territory with me. You can. There are moments for that. God gave Joshua an army of 600,000 earthly men. He gave me His entire host of army angels.

Friends, we are never alone.

He has victory for all of us on the other side of suffering. Jesus defeated sin, hell, and the grave. Why do we second guess what He will conquer in our lives? He wants every stone from every wall torn down.

Every stone will sing of what He can redeem.

I got home that afternoon and called a close mentor. Victory was won that day. I could literally feel myself stepping into land that He has promised for me.

Have circumstances changed? Not really.

But does the soil feel different? It really does. You may literally be an act of obedience away from entering your promised land.

As you pray for God to prosper that which has hurt you the most in this world, you will feel Him returning the years that were stolen. He may not ask you to "go for a run with Him" and circle your deepest place of pain. But He will ask you to seek the welfare of where He has you. He will ask you to bless those who have hurt you and to pray for those who have mistreated you. He will prove that He can be found in places just like these, in soil just like this.

He wants to give us promised land! It may require us to go through the wilderness to get there. But it awaits! He wants to take you there.

He is rebuilding every damaged space inside your heart. He is tearing down every high thing that exalts itself above Him. All these years that felt like silence weren't wasted. He is trading every trauma and giving us vantages of His grace in its place. Just like Joshua, the victories that God has for us are not deliverance for *just* us. It is fruit for everyone in our midst. Joshua's obedience was for all of Israel. It was for an entire remnant of people. Your obedience is for more than *just* you. Your obedience is for an entire remnant of people, too. When we view our victories as generational, we have eyes to see that our deliverance is not *just* for us. It's promised land for all that come after us.

God promised the Israelites that land. The fall of the walls of Jericho is a great reminder that God fulfills what He promises. Regardless of how much time passes, God will always make good on His promises.

It is a new season.

There is a new freedom. All that appeared to be lost, He has found and made better. Nothing is wasted!

Take hold of the only hand that is worthy. When we know that our hand is being held by the One who:

- Protects
- Guides
- Comforts
- Strengthens
- Sustains
- Heals
- Renews
- Redeems
- Restores
- Resurrects
- Delivers
- Loves
- Saves and knows ALL things

THEN, I can walk with confidence. Only then can I find purpose where He has me. Only then can I feel secure when He is holding my hand. 'Cause I can't even walk without Him holding my hand.

REFLECT

- There is a deep richness to be found in holding onto the hand of God and never letting go. Are you willing and ready to live with that kind of dependency?
- God desires to deliver us from everything that is keeping us from stepping into His land of promise for us. God told Joshua that He would give him victory if Joshua would: carry His presence, circle what needed to be torn down, and declare God's praise. What walls are standing in your way today?
- How can you carry His presence, circle those walls, and declare His praise?
- We can love His Word and not live His Word. How can you live out God's word in your life and circumstances?
- God commands us to seek the welfare of the places where He has us. How are you continuing to do that in this season?

SCRIPTURE

> The loyal walk in step with God. God blazes their path.
> If He stumbles, He is not down for long; God has a grip
> on His hand.
> Psalm 37:23

PRAYER

God, you take delight in establishing the way that I should go. You are keeping me from falling. You are guiding me to promised land. You help me to set my heart on things above. Thank You for leading me towards deeper flourishing. You uphold me through every season. I commit my life to Your will and Your way. In Jesus' name, Amen.

CHAPTER TWENTY
His Touch

Several years ago, when our daughter was only about two years old, she would often run up to me with a bottle of nail polish and point to her nails, asking me to paint her on some "pwutties." Every single time, her lack of patience interrupted and disrupted the work I was trying to do.

As she would run off, looking at her smudged, half-completed nails, I would ponder in my heart all the ways that her impatience has mirrored mine. She was content, momentarily, with incomplete work. I could see myself through her actions, and it brought great sorrow to my soul.

I wonder how often I have forfeited the best of what God has for me because I was satisfied and content with "good enough."

I wonder how often my inability to practice patience and trust interrupts the supernatural that God has planned for me.

I wonder how often I trample over the greatness of what He desires to do in my life because I'm not fully living in the moment or season where He has me, ultimately missing out on the completed work of God in my life.

I wonder how often I come to Him to ask Him to "do" something for me while missing the awe-struck opportunity of just basking in who He is.

Coming as a recipient, asking God to do something for me doesn't ultimately leave me changed. However, being in His presence and being made into His likeness–that changes me!

Through these seasons, even the painful places, as I have lingered in His presence, He has been faithful to replant a field of peace in my heart. It is not the "pwutties" that I needed from Him. It's the touch of His presence that I needed. It's the touch from the Gardener's hand over our lives that we need, but it isn't always what we want. *One of the major areas that I was finally able to surrender, in order to flourish, was letting go of what I wanted it to look like in order to have Him.*

There came a point where John 3:30 became real for me. I knew that I could experience more of His presence if I would surrender more.

John 3:30 says,

> He must increase, but I must decrease.

This verse is not hard to understand in theory. If we want more of God, we have to be willing for there to be less of us. There's not enough room for us and God to both sit enthroned. John 3:30 can be hard to implement if we are selfish. It can be hard to implement if we need all the control. It can be hard to implement if we don't trust Him.

Remember back to the Israelites living in captivity in Babylon, in the midst of the most undesirable soil? Jeremiah told them that they would live under this captivity for 70 years! He instructed them to stay, settle down, marry, build houses, and plant gardens. By this, they knew their exile wouldn't be a short stay. The soil would likely feel undesirable most days. It's not what they had in mind for their future, and it sure wasn't what they wanted it to look like. In the midst of all of this news that felt crushing, Jeremiah also then told them:

> Seek the welfare of the city where
> I have sent you into exile.
> Jeremiah 29:7

The word "seek" in Hebrew is "lechapeesh," which means to search, crave, and hunt for. The word "welfare" is the Hebrew word "shalom." It means physical, emotional, spiritual, and financial peace and prosperity. His

Word does not say to simply seek the welfare of *any* soil. It says to seek the welfare of the one where God sent you.

There's a difference.

One you choose. The other is the one that God chooses for you.

Jeremiah instructed them, from the Lord, to *crave* the physical, emotional, spiritual, and financial peace of this city where they were sent. This city could easily have become the root of bitterness in their lives. God knew that. Even so, He instructed them to hunt down peace. He commanded them to flourish where He sent them. He commands the same for us, even if the environments aren't what we would choose. These words were spoken to the Israelites in the midst of hardship and suffering; people who were likely desiring immediate rescue and escape. Some of them could not embrace the enduring hardship enough to see what He had for them in it. They just wanted their nails painted.

Not many of us can say that we have been held captive for 70 years, but God may ask us to endure seasons, places, and circumstances that feel like exile soil spaces. Everything about where God has you may feel like a displacement. It may include wilderness roads that are lonely, harsh, full of rejection, and saturated in abuse that you don't understand.

Honestly speaking, the majority of my thoughts, in my own Babylon season, were radically different from the command that Jeremiah gave to the exiles. He told them to seek welfare. He told them to crave peace and pray for the prosperity of a place that felt harmful.

I found myself desiring justice, wanting every wrong made right.

As the Lord is pruning us, it becomes evidently clear that He is giving us the same command that Jeremiah was giving the Israelites. There are days when that command will feel unfair.

How is it possible to pray for people who have hurt you deeply?

How is it possible to pray for God to enrich the soil underneath your feet when it's the soil that has caused you your deepest pain?

How is it possible to crave peace for a place that has held you captive?

We have become a culture that teaches us to stay far away from toxic or unsafe people. We have concluded that those who love us and treat us well deserve our best love. We build protective barriers around ourselves, keeping out anyone and anything that does not make us feel good about ourselves. We act with self-preservation in mind. Our culture says this is freedom, but in reality, it only reveals our shallow roots and how weak we truly are. It reveals our lack of good fruit. It is a fear response, believing that we are too fragile and easily influenced by the nature of another. It reveals that Jesus is not more in our lives. It reveals that He has become less, and we have remained more. It reveals our lack of flourishing.

Imagine if we all lived according to Jesus' teaching? As a believer in Jesus Christ, we are to be fruit bearers. We have been called to exemplify love, joy, peace, patience, kindness, goodness, faithfulness, gentleness, and self-control in all seasons of our lives—even those seasons that feel like winter; even when we feel like we are being burned off completely; even in the exile soil spaces. We have not been called to bear fruit and seek peace and welfare only in rich soil.

We are called to take sacrificial love into broken hearts and broken spaces.

We are called to take sacrificial love into the hearts of those who have broken ours.

There may be unique situations where boundary lines must be drawn in radically abusive situations that are dangerous. Boundaries may very well be necessary in your life! God will help give you the discernment, guidance, and wisdom that you need for those situations. I'm not referencing those types of abusive and dangerous situations. I'm talking about people, situations, and circumstances that aren't our preference. I am talking about loving those that are not easy to love, but we can.

Friends, we can.

God's desire was to teach the Israelites that their hope, identity, and security couldn't be found outside of Him. He wanted them rooted in the knowledge of who He was and who they were in Him, so firmly, in fact, that their circumstance and setting did not derail them from what He was doing and who they were becoming. *If we aren't careful, we can come under the influence of our circumstances.* But if we choose to trust the move of His hand over our lives, we can flourish in these seasons.

Every instruction from God holds purpose, and it's usually three-fold: for His glory, for our betterment, and for the expansion of His Kingdom on earth. He taught them patience, and it taught them where their hope was found. Yes, God put the Israelites in exile, and He did it to drive them back to Him. He wanted their roots to drink from His living water. He wanted them to learn to seek Him and put their hope in Him and nothing else.

The entire story is full of this glorious hope of the fulfillment of God's promises to His people. God had a long-term plan for their salvation and future.

Looking back, from a more healed perspective, I can see how He had a long-term plan for me, too. To receive the removal I was seeking would have meant trading away the experience gained and, in doing so, would have disrupted the very method God was using to bring me to flourishing.

I was impatient in His presence, too, just like my daughter. I became an expert at disrupting all that He had for me. I wanted God to do a work and to do it quickly. I became content with incomplete and unfinished work over and over again in my life.

Metaphorically speaking, my nails were smudged for years!

I came running to Him, knowing I needed something. I wanted to be changed. I did. I wanted to look different. I thought the way to transformation and healing was going to be quick, but the route to truly being healed is found by being in His presence.

God is continually trying to teach us to take hold of a hope that is not attached to what we are going through.

His word in Jeremiah tells us that He can be found in soil just like this: when rescue and escape are what we want, but finding Him fully is what we need. We are told in Jeremiah that He is a findable God:

> You will seek me and find me
> when you seek (crave) me with your whole heart.
> Jeremiah 29:13

In my exile season, I was seeking the Lord. I was. However, I wasn't giving him everything. I wasn't always abiding. I wasn't trusting Him with the painful parts. In fact, I blamed Him for not removing me and rescuing me from it. I gave Him the pieces of my heart that were comfortable for me to give up, and I complained and grieved the rest. There are many who seek the Lord. Few seek Him and offer Him their entire heart. A full surrender is what God desires.

Whether you come by brokenness naturally or you choose to walk into it, it provides the opportunity to drive you to our Maker…if you let it.

the path to flourishing may not have been what I wanted, but it's what He knew I needed.

Our brokenness and deficiencies oftentimes are the very environments that break up the soil for us to seek Him in a deeper and more desperate way. It allows us to see our brokenness and deficiencies as a gift.

I have been given the gift to see the Master Gardener's hand and to feel His tender touch over my life. He has shown me the richness of all that He has for me. It wasn't what I wanted from Him all those years ago, but it's what He knew I needed. His presence has become the treasure I now desire more than anything else. It's His touch that I know I have to have to live and breathe.

There is one hero in the Bible who has inspired me in ways that truly feel unmatched. She is so heroic that she isn't even named. But she's the one who taught me what it looks like to touch Jesus in ways that lead to triumph.

She's a woman who, with bleeding guts, still had enough to touch Jesus when everything about her life felt upside down.

This woman, who again has no name, had suffered from a bleeding condition for 12 years. She had depleted every coin of her finances trying to be made well by doctors. She was left hopeless, helpless, and isolated. No money and no friends. She was told that she shouldn't even be in the crowd. She was deemed "unclean." Back in those times, women like this weren't allowed in the camps, the synagogues, or in temples. They were thrust into isolation, forbidden to touch anything or anyone. It was custom that if they touched a Rabbi or any holy person and made that person unclean, it would result in their death. The type of death for this kind of act was death by stoning.

Coming into the crowd that day seemed scandalous to many. This unnamed woman crawled in desperation through a clamoring crowd. The account of this "certain woman" is found in Mark 5:25-34. There's a portion that stands out to me:

> She came up behind Him in the crowd and touched the fringe of His garment. She thought, "If I could just touch the hem of His garment, I know I will be healed."

She fought through everything to get to Jesus: the crowd, every whisper around her, perhaps even disgust and mockery, and she pressed in to touch the fringe of His garment. The word "touch" in Hebrew is "hepsato," which means "to fasten to, to lay hold of, or to attach oneself to." The word "fringe" in Hebrew is "kraspedou," which means "a margin."

This sentence in the Hebrew states more clearly this way: *She came up behind Jesus in the crowd and attached herself to a piece of Him.*

She touched a single thread of Him, not even His fullness.

In her desperation, this unclean woman attached herself to the One that she knew could heal her. Even in a lowly position, she fastened her focus on Him and caught hold of the slightest fringe of His garment.

A single thread of Jesus healed her that day!

Imagine what having all of Him could do.

Are we willing to push past and through every pain, person and distraction in our lives to touch Him?

In this scandalous and risky act, this woman wasn't just reaching out to touch the fringe of Jesus' garment; she was also proclaiming that she had faith in Jesus, so much so that she risked her very life. The very moment she touched Him, He knew it. There is nothing unknown to Him.

We will never touch Jesus, and Him be unaware.

We will never receive, even just a margin of Him, and be unchanged.

Jesus told this woman that her faith healed her. According to the customs of that time, they didn't believe that Jesus should have been able to even continue to travel and heal the sick after this. What the religious elite didn't know was that the holiness of Jesus trumps everything in our lives that is wrong, messy, and unclean. Her uncleanliness was no match for Jesus. She didn't even have to barely touch Him to be healed.

Similarly, things that have impaired us for years are no match for Jesus. Pain that has haunted us our entire lives can be healed in a single moment with Jesus. Any deficiency that we have is no match for Jesus. A single touch from Him can heal us. A margin of His presence is enough.

It's His touch that healed her that day. We know that.

Jesus also said it was her faith that healed her.

He didn't say that it was her position that healed her. She didn't have one.

He didn't say it was her last name. It was never even recorded.

He didn't say it was everything she'd ever done for Him that healed her.

He said it was her faith that healed her.

Jesus' love for us isn't reduced to or elevated by human standards or labels. His love for us is so-that all we have to do is reach out and touch Him in faith.

We have to know that we need His touch more than anything else in this world. We must be desperate enough to sacrifice anything and everything to position ourselves to touch Him and stay rooted in Him. I'm not sure there's a posture more desperate than crawling through a crowd where you aren't welcome. I'm not sure there's a more desperate and humble posture than roots diving into the ground for their source of life and sustenance.

If we want Him, we have to want the things that are getting in the way less.

Over time, through my healing process, I began to fully realize that it was Him that I had to have. If it's Him that we have, we will do anything, and it will be our delight to do it, not because it looks like what we thought it would. It's the way of the Lord, oftentimes. The very thing we think it will look like is often the opposite. The very things I thought I needed were the very things He chose not to give me.

Do you think the woman with the issue of blood wanted to be shamed and isolated in this way for 12 years? I'm sure it was painful and lonely. We know it was long-lasting. But would His touch have meant as much if she wasn't desperate for it? Would she have even been on her knees crawling at all?

The things in our lives that we can't make sense of and don't understand are the overflow of His lavishing mercy and grace. There have been seasons in my life where I've felt God say: **"I'm going to hold onto this until you don't want it anymore."** Sometimes we are praying to God and asking Him to give us something that He knows won't draw us closer to Him. Perhaps we need to be in a season of deficiency so that we will get desperate enough to crawl on our knees through a crowd to touch Him with real faith.

If there's any part of you that is longing for things to look a different way, any part of you that has been clinging to a certain interpretation of what you think a flourished life would look like, you'll be amazed at what happens when you stop looking at it—and you start looking at Jesus. Living in a state of flourishing allows us to see adversity differently.

Instead of asking God, "Why do You have me here? What are You doing," we can instead say, "Wow! What a privilege to be woven into the threads of releasing Your glory!"

Trust in the slow work of God. We can be people who are naturally impatient in everything to reach the end quicker. We often want to skip the intermediate stages. We grow impatient of being "on the way" to something unknown and something new.

And yet, it is the way of progress. The beauty is in the becoming.

It is made by passing through some stages of instability. Be planted and pruned without fighting and undoing the process. Only God can say and know what this new life, gradually forming within you, will become.

We were created to worship Him and to boast in Him—to reveal His power in the midst of every weakness within. You can be sure to see Him, and when He's filled your gaze, you'll be blown away when He brings you the very thing you quit caring about if you had or not because He has so satisfied you. The desires of our hearts begin to change when we delight in Him.

When He becomes everything to you, this promise is made manifest in your life.

> I will be found by you, and I will bring you back from captivity. I will gather you from all the places where I banished you, and I will bring you back to the place from which I carried you into exile.
> Jeremiah 29:14 (emphasis mine)

He will always bring us out of our captivity and exile if we stay rooted in Him. This fulfilled promise in Jeremiah may look literal in your life. Sometimes we are physically brought out. He truly may move you out of your place of captivity. I know that will come with great relief and celebration. Other times, He will ask you to remain, but He changes your heart and vision. You may still be in the same soil, but the soil is beginning to feel drastically different now. The fulfillment of the promise in our lives is that we choose not to see it as exile anymore. We are no longer in undesirable soil. We are sovereignly arranged. We can have a vision like that when we choose to see Him alone. He is enough. He is more than enough.

The miracle, for me, isn't that He removed me from exile. The miracle is that He changed me without having to.

The strength of my soul was born on the backs of moments that brought me to my knees. For me, the promise of new life was on the other side of suffering. The broken pieces of my heart are starting to heal on the very same soil that shattered them. I'm exchanging doubt for truth, blindness for sight, joy for sorrow, and ashes for beauty. Where it took me from to where it took me to, I'd do it again. If we knew what God knows, we'd ask for exactly what He gives. He gives good gifts.

He has plans to prosper us. To give us hope and a future. He is with us in every step of the journey–mending every fracture, healing every wound, and restoring every lost hope where we were once shattered. The next time you walk through a valley, you may recognize it as such, but it won't destroy you, because you have deep roots in Him.

You are flourishing in Him.

When you walk through the valley, you will know it is not your punishment. It is for your betterment. He may not physically remove you from your place of exile, but He will allow you to flourish there.

Our God is a good Gardener who isn't just found in the valleys; He's the one who wants to walk through them with us. He works in ways that we will never know. Sometimes the pathway to your flourishing will be a mystery, but it will happen. The Gardener won't leave us unfinished. He won't abandon the work of His hands. He is restoring you. He is healing you. He is rebuilding you.

When you begin to thrive and flourish, you are going to look around, and it's going to be the richest and sweetest soil your feet have ever touched.

REFLECT

- God was continually trying to teach the Israelites to experience a hope and identity found in Him. He was desperate for them to take hold of a hope that wasn't attached to what they were going through. He wanted to be found by them. Reflect on how you have found Him as you've put your hope in Him and sought Him wholeheartedly.
- The woman who crawled to be healed by Jesus was said to have been healed because of her faith. The promise of new life is sometimes on the other side of suffering. Do we have the faith and humility to crawl to get to Him and experience new life?
- His promise to us is even more than just rebuilding! The evidence of the flourishing one is the one whose lips never stop singing the praises of the One who redeemed and rebuilt them. How can you praise Him today for all that He has done in your life?

SCRIPTURE

> From them will come songs of thanksgiving
> and the sound of rejoicing!
> Jeremiah 30:19

PRAYER

God, I want to seek You with my whole heart. I want to know You with my whole mind. I want to pursue You everyday. Help me to seek after You wholeheartedly. I am not ashamed to crawl through a crowd to get to You. Everything besides You can be a distraction. I need Your touch in my life. Reveal Yourself to me and allow me to hear Your voice. My hope is in You and You alone. In Jesus' name, amen.

CHAPTER TWENTY-ONE
Manasseh & Ephraim

At the beginning of the pruning section, we were introduced to a terrified refugee named Jacob. God appeared to him in his shattered and messy circumstances and passed along every promise He had for Jacob. The night Jacob laid his head upon a rock became a marker in his life. It became the place where God met with Him. It was the place where He was anointed by God. In one of the most distressed, terrified, and lonely spaces that Jacob had ever found himself in was the exact place that became a marker in his life of revelation, assurance, and promise.

Jacob went on to have 12 sons, one of whom was Joseph. Joseph endured a lot of hardship and affliction throughout his lifetime. He was rejected. His family betrayed him. He was falsely accused and forgotten about, sitting in a prison cell and still being faithful there. Thirteen years of toil and affliction occurred before Joseph ever saw the fruitful abundance of what God had for him. God never left Him. God had something for Joseph even when Joseph couldn't see it. There was a flourishing to be found in the affliction. Remember, there's always a remnant left after affliction if we have eyes to see it.

Joseph was eventually exalted to a high position by God and ended up being the conduit that saved an entire nation from famine. In a time when famine was everywhere and grain was scarce, Joseph was one of the very few who had access to every source of grain. As the famine grew worse, many were sent to Egypt, where Joseph was, to get more grain.

About 22 years had passed since Joseph was sold into slavery by his family, who had betrayed him. It isn't surprising that they didn't recognize him. The ones who betrayed Joseph the most were now the very ones standing in front of him, needing grain just to live. The one they sold into slavery now had the power of life and death over them!

Joseph could have used this opportunity to get even. But that's not who Joseph was. Joseph had godly humility. Instead of allowing his betrayers to perish, Joseph fed them. He welcomed them in. He arranged a place for them to live in a nearby land. They lived in the comfort of his Shalom, welfare and peace.

Joseph knew how to "seek the welfare" of the place where God had him. He understood what Shalom meant.

Shalom is the end of hostilities and war, as much as it depends on us. It is making and keeping peace. It is a right relationship with God and God's creation. Flourishing is the benefit of Shalom. Shalom restores everything back to God's original design.

Like Joseph, those who have hurt you may come to you to get grain. Joseph was able to bring sustenance and life to those who betrayed him and hurt him. Are you?

Joseph underwent such depths of affliction that he coined this profound statement:

> You intended to harm me, but God intended it for good,
> to accomplish (method God used) what is now being done.
> Genesis 50:20

God blessed Joseph and gave two sons: Manasseh and Ephraim. He called the firstborn, Manasseh, and said, "For the Lord has made me to **forget** all my pain." And to the youngest, Ephraim, "For the Lord has made me to be **fruitful** in the land of my affliction."

For me to flourish is to live a life of Mannasseh and Ephraim. *Mannasseh* is a daily choice. It's a daily surrender. Asking the Lord to make us forget all of our pain is a cross we bear, and a gift He wants to give. He *will* renew our minds if we keep surrendering. It doesn't mean that what happened to us isn't real. It doesn't mean that it never happened. It just means that it's over. It means that we don't require people to take accountability before we heal. We have to refuse to place that lordship into the hands of another. We already have a Lord, and He has set us free.

For us to flourish is to live a life of *Ephraim*, to declare that God has made us to be fruitful in the land of our affliction. Friends, if the Lord can make us fruitful in the land of our affliction, we can be fruitful anywhere and through anything

Sometimes the afflictions in the wilderness are of our own making. Sometimes the afflictions that happen in the wilderness are of God's choosing. Every time, the afflictions that happen in the wilderness are the place of transformation. It's the method of bearing sweet fruit.

Nobody chooses affliction, yet God is gracious, and He is purposeful. He's so gracious, in fact, that He can take even what the enemy meant to destroy us, and He can use it for our good. Every wilderness is for our betterment. Every wilderness is for our flourishing.

The Lord blessed Joseph and gave him two gifts, and I believe He wants to give us those same two offspring gifts! He wants to make us forget all of our pain, and He wants us to be fruitful even in affliction. His Word says:

> Forget (Mannasseh) the former things; do not dwell on
> the past. See, I am doing a new thing (Ephraim)!
> Do you not see it?
> Isaiah 48:18-20 (emphasis mine)

We don't have to see through the lens of what happened to us forever. Healing is our portion. Restoration is our portion. Do we believe it?

Ephraim and Manasseh went on to become two of the most powerful tribes in the nation. They flourished. My harvest of flourishing was found when I took my eyes off everything around me. When I quit looking for the harvest where I believed the harvest should be growing, I could hear God singing over me, "Melia, do you not see how you are flourishing? Do you not see how by Me stretching you, you are producing more fruit than ever before? My child, this is the harvest! This is where the flourishing is!"

Sometimes the harvest we were looking for was never meant to grow.

Sometimes the harvest we are looking for was never meant to grow. Sometimes the harvest is found in the growth of peace in our hearts, endurance in the brutal race, contentment in the trials, acceptance in the loss, and joy in the journey. If we really want to see a harvest, all we have to do is look in the mirror.

Think how far you've come.

Each day that you hold fast to God and stand in the midst of struggle, a bounty is growing. When this happens, a magnificent thing takes place: You stop looking for your harvest all around you, because you have learned that the harvest is within you.

Every time the enemy tries to get you to remember, tell him you forgot. Every time you remember, forgive again. Choose it again and again. Even if what happened happened years ago.

Every time you remember, forget.

Every time you remember, forgive.

We can choose not to remember.

He is doing a new thing. Do you see it?

REFLECT

- God gave Joseph two gifts: Mannasseh ("the Lord caused me to forget all my pain") and Ephraim ("the Lord made me to be fruitful in my affliction"). He wants to give you these two gifts, as well. Will you receive them?
- Look how far you have come, my friend! A bounty is growing in your midst. The harvest is within you. Take some time to reflect and journal how far God has brought you.

Ask God to help you forget all your pain. He is making you fruitful in every affliction. What He gave you to carry out, He gave to you and you alone. We shouldn't want to waste any more time. Let us stop disqualifying ourselves. We must quit telling God that He can't do the impossible through our lives! I don't want to let the miracles pass into the hands of the next generation. He can do the impossible through you!

SCRIPTURE

> I remain confident of this: I will see the goodness of the Lord
> in the land of the living.
>
> Psalm 27:13

PRAYER

God, thank You that what was meant to harm me, you're turning to my advantage. No weapon formed against me will prosper. Thank you that I will recover all that was lost. Help me to know You so well and to trust You so fully that fear and doubt have no place in my heart. I am in awe of the miracles that flow from Your righteous right Hand. You are my deliverer and the strength of my soul. You help me to do the impossible through You. I remain confident that I will see Your goodness in the land of the living. You are resurrecting dead things in my life. In Jesus' name, amen.

CHAPTER TWENTY-TWO

The Manna Lifestyle

Even in our flourishing, we will come up against challenges in this life. There is not a single strong oak and cedar tree that will be untouched by stiff winds and howling storms. There will still be tragedies and heartache. With Christ, we are now positioned and rooted to navigate these challenges, tragedies, and heartaches differently. Do we know how to *walk* in great difficulty?

It is inadequate for me to talk only about all of the flourishing that awaits and not talk about the resistance that will come because of what you now possess through Jesus Christ! You carry an anointing. You behold a calling. The enemy will come against you because of that, friends. Sometimes there's tension that we have to learn to navigate.

How do we live with joy and still bear fruit when resistance comes against us?

God didn't just anoint you for the assignment. He also anointed you for the attacks. The anointing of your life wasn't given to you for ease, but for endurance. The battles you face are not signs of failure, but rather confirmation of your calling. The enemy wouldn't attack what isn't a threat. God has equipped you with strength, wisdom, and discernment to overcome every opposition. You have deep roots drawing from His source and supply. Draw near to Him and stay rooted in His Word. When the attacks feel relentless, it's a sign of the potential and purpose that God has placed inside of you. The struggles you face aren't random—they reflect the weight of the mission God has entrusted to you and the greatness He put inside of you.

His Word in Psalm 23 says that He is the good Shepherd. This Psalm is full of promises. Here are a few:

He will lay us down in green pastures.

He will lead us beside still waters.

He will restore our souls.

He will lead us in the path of righteousness.

He promises to walk with us through the deepest valleys.

He will prepare a table before us in the presence of our enemies.

He will anoint our heads with oil.

His goodness and mercy will follow us all the days of our lives.

Someday, I'd love to write an entire book on just the promises to be found in Psalm 23. For now, I'd like to focus on the promise that He will lay us down in green pastures.

All these years, I've misunderstood "green pastures". I've always pictured a bounty of lavish fields near peaceful flowing streams. I was

listening to someone who had shared about their time visiting the Judean wilderness—the very place where David wrote Psalm 23. The visual geography was not endless meadows of grain. It was actually scattered grass along dry and dusty paths.

This is significant because the sheep had to depend upon their Shepherd for every meal. In the correct context of David's writing, grass would grow up in small collections of tasseled strands along dusty soil. The sheep could only eat a single bite, and then they would need to look to the Shepherd to direct them to their next mouthful. Without the leading of the Shepherd, the sheep would never reach their next mouthful. They did not take a step outside of the Shepherd's care.

Sounds a lot like my daughter, doesn't it?

Sounds a lot like Moses, too.

At the beginning of Psalm 23, David writes these words:

> The Lord is my Shepherd. I shall not want.

The Hebrew phrase for "I shall not want" is "lo eschar," which means: "Nothing will be missing from my life."

God doesn't always give you what you want. But He does give you everything you need. It's not always endless mouthfuls. Not excess for tomorrow. Not a shortage for today. It's enough for now. It is divine provision. Trusting the Shepherd to lead you means deep reliance. Trusting the Shepherd for your next mouthful of manna means that He guides when the path to get there is dusty.

When the grass is scattered, He leads.

When the resources and revelations feel scarce, He provides.

What if our "not enough" is actually God's "exactly what you need?"

What if our "doesn't make sense" is actually God's "exactly how it's supposed to be?"

God provided manna for the Israelites during their exodus journey. The Hebrew word for "manna" literally means, "what is it?" This bread-like substance that would appear each morning was a complex idea for the Israelites. How did it get there? What was it? Simply, it was daily provision. It was just what they needed. That's the beauty of His provision; it meets us exactly where we are and gives us exactly what we need.

When the path is blurry, direction arrives.

When resources dwindle, supply appears.

When strength fails, renewal is found. Right on time, every time.

If we want to flourish in every season and bear fruit through it all, we need to embrace the manna lifestyle. We have to learn to trust that God always has a fresh supply of everything that we might need for our tomorrows. The flourishing lifestyle is the one who has learned to be content in all circumstances and in all seasons. The "what is it" seasons may very well turn out to be "exactly what we needed."

What feels like exile may actually be our exodus.

God has a fresh supply of everything we might need for our tomorrows.

REFLECT

- How can you trust Him to provide for all things in this season?
- What if your "not enough" is exactly what you need?
- What if all that doesn't make sense is exactly how it is supposed to be?
- The Israelites looked at the provision of God and His manna and said, "what is this?" How can we stop living shocked that He is our provider of all things?

Take some time today and write down ways that He has provided for you over your life. Thank Him for working in ways you did not expect and in times you did not know He was.

SCRIPTURE

> The Lord is my Shepherd, I lack nothing.
> Psalm 23:1

PRAYER

God, Everything I need is everything You are. Your providence is what allows for my story not to be over. Thank You for opening my eyes to see Your provision that comes from You. I take possession. I receive it. I will drink from Your water. I will eat of Your manna—that is exactly what I need. Even when it doesn't make sense to me, I will trust that it is exactly as it should be. You are for me! Nothing will be missing from my life through You. In Jesus' name, amen.

CHAPTER TWENTY-THREE
Cedars of Lebanon

To live a flourishing life means that we grow or develop in a healthy or vigorous way, especially as the result of a particularly favorable environment. Not every environment or situation we are in will cater to us. Storms will come. Howling winds will try to tear at us. The beating of hot days will attempt to shrivel us. We need to get comfortable being uncomfortable if we want to flourish.

God is the Master Gardener of our souls. Only He has the ability to make our environments favorable, enrich the soil of our hearts, and shift our perspective.

Psalm 92:12 and 14-15 (emphasis mine) says,

> The righteous will flourish like the palm tree and will grow like a Cedar in Lebanon. They are planted in the house of the Lord; they will flourish in the courts of our God. They will still bear fruit in old age; they are full of sap and remain green, to declare that the Lord is upright.

The cedar of Lebanon is a mountain tree that grows in rocky soils in the highest place of Israel, at heights of about 1800m. They grow even where the soil is snow-impacted! They sometimes can take up to 25-30 years before they begin to flower or bloom.² Even so, in snow-filled soil, they still flourish. Even in the dead of winter, they live and flourish. Even in what feels like captivity, even in our Babylons, even in our pruning seasons, God says that we can grow like this. He has planted us. He has placed and positioned us. When we are rooted in Him, we will flourish. It's His promise over our lives.

The cedar trees that grow in the mountains of Lebanon should hold a very special meaning for us. The Bible mentions that Solomon used these very trees to build God's temple. Solomon had every resource available. He surpassed everyone in wealth and riches. He could have picked any wood that he wanted to build the Temple of the Lord, and he chose cedar.

DEEP ROOTS

The cedars of Lebanon have the *deepest roots* of nearly any other tree. For every 10 feet of height above ground, the roots go down nearly 30 feet underground. The Hebrew word for "cedar" is "'erez," which means "to be firm" or "firmness of roots." The Hebrew word for Cedar is related to the strength and persistence of its roots.

We will only ever grow as tall as we are rooted.

Paul encourages us to be "deeply rooted and grounded in love" in Ephesians 3:17. As the roots of the cedar wrap around the rocks, we must wrap around God, our Rock of Ages. What we wrap ourselves around will determine how much we can withstand. We can be more resilient than we ever thought possible when we are attached to Him. We can withstand difficult climates and recover quickly. We can spring back after an intense bending, when our roots are holding us to life.

SAP

Cedar trees have a substance in the tips of their roots that allows their roots to drill through the toughest of rocks and boulders. It's what allows for their deep-rootedness, no matter what the roots come up against. Their

---

² http://flowersinisrael.com/cedruslibani_page.htm

roots can penetrate past and through the hard things below the surface that the naked eye cannot see or anticipate.

The rocks of resistance may feel like they are in the way, but with the sap of God, they provide the opportunity for us to be on our way to Heaven's riverside. Friends, we can penetrate even the hardest hearts of those in our midst if our roots are grounded in God's love. We can pierce through really difficult things when our roots are rightly rooted.

The sap of cedar trees also serves as a repellent against all harm. Their structure and make-up have an internal resistance to destruction and infections. No pestilence can come against them. They have their own "armor of God."

One of my favorite promises of God's "sap" in my life is Psalm 91.

> Say this: God, you're my refuge. I trust in You and I'm safe! That's right—He rescues you from hidden traps, shields you from deadly hazards. His huge outstretched arms protect you—under them you're perfectly safe; His arms fend off all harm. Fear nothing—not wild wolves in the night, not flying arrows by day, not disease that prowls through the darkness, not disaster that erupts at high noon. You'll stand untouched, because God is your refuge. The High God is your very home. Evil can't get close to you, harm can't get through the door. He ordered His angels to guard you wherever you go. If you hold onto Me for dear life, I'll get you out of trouble. I'll give you the best care if you'll only get to know and trust Me. Call Me and I'll answer, I'll be at your side in bad times; I'll rescue you, then throw you a party. I'll give you a long life, and I'll give you a long drink of my salvation.
> Psalm 91, MSG

This kind of protection and treatment from God produces a sweet aroma. In Biblical times, sap was used to make an anointing oil. When applied to a person, it spoke of strength and was a testimony of wholeness and restoration! His sap in our lives continues to offer us wholeness and restoration, strength and beauty.

A WIDE REACH

These cedar branches span more than 50 feet. Do you remember Joseph—the one who chose to forget all of his pain, and the one who believed that God would bring fruitfulness from his affliction? Do you know what God had to say about Joseph? In Genesis 49:22-26, it says:

> Joseph is a fruitful vine—a vine near a spring. His branches run over walls. The archers bitterly attacked him and harassed him severely, yet his bow remained unmoved, and his arms stayed limber.

The life of Joseph was full of hardship, abandonment and betrayal. Even so, He is described by God as "a fruitful vine" that drank from *the* spring. He knew which spring would nourish him. He had found the hidden spring. Joseph relied on God through every trial and triumph. In Biblical times, a vine was used as a metaphorical term for abundance and blessing. It sometimes takes 25-30 years for a cedar tree to bloom and bear fruit. In the same way, it may take time before you ever see the abundant flourishing of what God is doing in this season of your life, but He promises that if you stay attached to Him, a flourishing will happen.

This scripture says of Joseph that his branches ran over walls. There was nothing and no one too far for Joseph to reach towards and bless. He provided shade for the very people in his life who had hurt him the deepest. They were blessed under the comfort and shade of his wide-spread branches. His environments weren't favorable as we would define favor. However, He was able to bear fruit and flourish in some of the most harsh environments that we could ever imagine.

It's not the environments that make our lives favorable; it's being rooted in the One who enriches them that makes them favorable. With God's help, we can remain unmoved when the enemy surrounds us. We can overcome barriers and extend our influence as He blesses us. We can scale walls that we never thought were imaginable.

We will only ever grow as tall as we are rooted.

VANTAGE POINT

The trunk diameter of a cedar is over 8 feet, and it is not uncommon for these trees to reach as high as 150 feet tall! This type of vantage point is something that we can experience, friends.

In the very early stages of writing this book, my husband and I took a day off work to spend with our daughter on her school field trip to the zoo. My 6.3" husband could easily spot the animals first. He would point

them out so that our daughter could see them. Nearly every time, she would arch her back in frustration, outstretch her neck in determination, and say, "I still can't see them." My husband, then, hoisted her up onto his shoulders and gave her a better vantage point.

We have missed some of the most amazing things that God wants us to see and experience because we have been spiritually stunted.

But no longer.

We are rising up.

We are cedars of Lebanon placed in the highest peak of the tallest mountains. He is mounting us up!

His Word in Isaiah 40 promises that He will renew our strength and mount us up on wings like eagles. He is giving us a new position. He is giving us a new perspective.

When we are rooted and remain in Him, He will hoist us up onto His Holy shoulders and let us see all that He has. Everything that we couldn't see will be fully seen through His vantage point. Everything that didn't make sense will be full of revelation. Every lack will be fulfilled.

Every trauma has been traded for vantages of grace.

His goodness will wash over every valley pain below. We will see all that He's been doing there and thank Him for it.

GROWING IN UNITY

The limbs of the cedar trees often grow into the foliage of the neighboring trees. It is not uncommon for them to grow together as one. The way they choose to grow speaks of unity. Even if one tree becomes weak, its limbs are sustained due to the merging of life around it.

They don't compete with one another. They know they need one another in order to grow and flourish. The birds of the sky nestle in and wild animals give life under its branches.

We are to be a resting place for the weary ones in our midst. Our outstretched branches of abundance may be the very place where new life is born. What we overcame is now the life source for someone else who is buried.

SEEKING HIDDEN SPRINGS

Cedars grow downwards where their roots manage to seek hidden springs. Our life has found this hidden spring of God. Anything we touch, everything we encounter has to change for our good and for His glory. Everything has been hydrated by Heaven's riverside.

We are moving forward and we are moving upward.

We are flourishing in our homes, our churches, our jobs, and our communities.

Nothing can stand up against us.

From now forward, our lives will be watered abundantly. When the springs from the living God become the source from which we drink, we will be extraordinarily set apart! We are no longer dependent upon man to quench our thirst. We don't lack any good thing anymore. Nothing is withheld from us! Nothing will be missing from our lives! He is leading us beside the still waters. No more pollution will be ingested! His promise is that we will dwell in the house of the Lord forever.

Everything that we lost, He's giving it back!

The worth that was lost, is given back to us!

The joy that was lost, is coming back!

Every single thing that got robbed is being given back!

He will restore our souls!!! There is no power and no thing that can overcome God! When God purposefully plants you, nothing can come against it. Nothing can come against the flourishing that He has for us. The

It's His presence that turns valleys into meadows of fruitfulness.

planting of the Lord is going to give you a vantage point that you've never experienced before.

God planted cedars in Lebanon as a sign of His power and goodness. The cedars of Lebanon were a gift from God. God could have chosen any place to make His dwelling, and He chose you. Our lives are a gift from God to be used for God. Our very lives are to be a blessing to those around us. We are a living witness of the living God on this earth. We are not here to just exist. We are to be strong in storms. We are to bear fruit in every season as we are planted in living water. We are bearing the fruitfulness of a living God to generations!

When we begin to see purpose where He has planted us, have grown deep roots, been pruned by His tender Hand, and have experienced the flourishing effects of His treatment and care, we see everything differently. It's His presence that turns valleys into meadows of fruitfulness. It's His presence that turns hard-rock wildernesses into revelations of promises. He is our Master Gardener. He can take what feels like a wasteland, breathe on it, and it becomes a well-watered garden.

That's what His care over our lives has the power to do.

If we plant ourselves in God's house, we will flourish in His courts. He is the Master Gardener and caretaker of our souls. We are promised to flourish under His care. As His righteousness, we are planted, set by faith, watered by the Word, rooted in Christ, and therefore will flourish–be green and vigorous in the courts of our God.

We can be standing on the very same soil that once felt abusive, and it now feel abundant.

This is our song of triumph and portion:

> They will come and shout for joy. They will rejoice
> in the bounty of the Lord. They will be like a well-
> watered garden.
> Jeremiah 31:12

Friends, I am miles from where I was, and yet, so far from where I want to be. I guess that's the beauty of becoming. It's progress, not perfection. Not the finish line but the journey.

God found *David* in a pit of destruction and turned him into a ruling King after God's own heart. He never left him.

He found *Moses* in all of his insecurities, set His feet on Holy ground, and entrusted Him with the 10 commandments. Even while Moses allowed people around him to sway him, God still chose to use him in remarkable ways.

He came upon the bitter, *paralyzed man at the pool* and turned him into a believer. The man's life was forever changed.

God met *Jacob* in his running and gave him revelation for a lifetime. He blessed his family for generations.

He pursued the *woman at the well* in all of her brokenness and thirst and hydrated her by His living water. He restored her soul. She went from nameless to a witness in one encounter.

God found *Hagar*, beat down, rejected, and left behind by the most influential people in her life, and He turned her into the mother of a great nation. He saw her.

Ezekiel, standing in a valley surrounded by dead bodies, watched God resurrect them back to life. He witnessed the very breath of God bring back the dead. Nothing is too far gone!

The *three Hebrew boys* who sat in the fire because of their faith came face to face with their Deliverer. He was with them.

Joshua, a faithful one, got to lead the Israelites into the promised land because of His courage. His life is a selfless testimony. God used him.

The power of God touched *the unclean woman* who had lived for 12 years being shunned and denied. Even still, she was unapologetically on the hunt for Him. He healed her and rewarded her faith.

God saw *Joseph* through betrayal, slavery, and prison. He elevated Him to a high position and gave him back all that was stolen. He showed favor to him.

God stayed with *the Israelites* through all of their idolatry, unbelief, sin, and complaining. He allowed circumstances and hardship to change their heart. He did as He promised and He brought them out of their captivity and to the Promised Land. He chose them.

God led His sinless son, ***Jesus,*** through the wilderness, into a brutal and earthly death. He never left Him. He raised Him from the dead and positioned Him at His right hand, to forever be the one who intercedes for us and captures our prayers! He loved Him.

He never leaves us.

He sees us.

He changes us.
He delivers us.
He brings us out of our captivity.
He restores us.
He heals us.
He uses us.
He blesses us.
He elevates us.
He gives us favor.
He rewards us.
He loves us.
He could've chosen any place to make His home, and He chose *you*.
He can do all things.

These stories are the very proof that we are purposefully placed. Our stories can be messy, but they are also beautiful. Where you are right now is not the end of the story. *You* are purposefully placed. Every season holds purpose, purposes to magnify the greatness of God, to show others He is Mighty. Every season provides purpose to lift us out of our trenches, to stretch our roots, to strengthen our branches in order for others to perch under the comfort of our Shalom. These seasons give purpose to further His kingdom through our hurt, our victories, our pain, and our triumphs.

There is purpose in the undesirable, to flourish in His righteousness.

From seeds found in undesirable soil to a flourishing life that comes only from being tethered to His vine. It's a journey of growth. It's an invitation to take hold of the beauty in the becoming.

Flourishing is *joy in the journey* and *contentment in every circumstance.* It's learning the treasure of staying attached to Him through every high and in every low.

One day we'll look back at the full picture with renewed clarity. Living in a state of flourishing is birthed in an eagerness to praise Him in any and all circumstances. It is the melody of our hearts to articulate our gratitude to Him through the worship of our lives.

Unwavering adoration. Anthems of praise.

For you are purposefully placed.

You are rooted and restored.

F – Forgive
L – Love
O – Offering
U – Unwavering
R – Reliance
I – Inhabit
S – Sanctuary
H – Hope
I – Intentional
N – Nourish
G – Gratitude

Acrostic created by Marcie Harryman

To you who aspires deeper roots.
To you who is willing & ready
to live this flourishing life.
To you -- my friend,

A journal entry for the journey:

When you find yourself tipped over by the storms of life, when you feel like all that remains is shattered pieces, you will find a God who has met you there. He won't walk past you or around all the brokenness. He isn't afraid to step into shattered spaces. He will pick up your broken bits, every single one, and He will restore you back to wholeness. Every fallen piece will find its purpose.

Nothing takes more courage & faith than giving God permission to pick up every piece and allow Him to use it the way He chooses.

Oftentimes, our very own stories -- most especially the painful parts, are the very ingredients God uses to break us open for His use.

It is a privilege & an honor to be broken open in such a way.

My prayer is that you would always see the precious gift of being an instrument in the hands of the Almighty & all-knowing God.

If your life could leave a legacy, may it be: Lo echsar --

In him, nothing will be missing from my life.

You can search the whole world and you'll never find anyone who cares for you like Jesus.

You'll never know another who will fulfill you the way that Jesus does. Amidst dark days, His grace is sufficient -- it's all you need.

Each step is part of the journey. Not every step will feel glamorous, but it's purposeful.

What you are going through will one day become what He's brought you through.

Remain on the narrow path.
Press on toward the upward call.
Stay steadfast in patience.

He is continually guiding you
to higher & holier ground.

Stay attached to Him.
Learn the gift of being rightly
rooted.

The care of His Hand over your
life is one of redemption &
restoration.

There is favor in the flames.
There are remnants from the ruins.

Let it be known -
    Through every season & in every
    circumstance ... that your
    joy is found in Christ alone.

Your story, no matter what it looks like,
is the most honest & powerful testimony
that you have to the greatness of God.

    Never stop telling it.

Your friend & encourager in Christ,

 Melia

Acknowledgments

Writing this book felt like a dream that was too far away. It's something that I have held in my heart for a lot of years, uncertain where to even start. What began as a compilation of all of my favorite devotions that I've written over the years, turned into an unraveling of my own story. One that I didn't see coming. What felt like feathers flying in a windstorm, was God holding the pen of my heart and making something beautiful through the ink. So much of this book was for me. God gave me the opportunity to walk hand in hand with Him through layers of healing that I didn't realize I still needed. I knew it would mean being vulnerable and open to surprises around any and every bend. It turned out to be all of those things times a hundred. It wouldn't have been made possible without those in my life who were willing to step into the deep waters with me.

Jeremy—my steady, better half. In a lot of ways, this is your story, too. You've shown me how to deliver our story with grace and mercy. You've held my story and my heart well. You were the very first investment. I remember the day you came home to find me swimming in papers and you handed me an organizing binder. Thank you for believing in me and allowing it to be used for His glory.

Our kids—Hunter, Case and Hattie Pearl. You were patient to allow our dining room table to be scattered with endless papers and sticky notes for nearly 2 years and never complained. "It's mom's book stuff." Thank you for sacrificing so that this "book stuff" could come to fruition. I've grown to know God deeper through motherhood. Thank you for giving me that gift. As each day passes, and I see you towering over me, I am reminded how fleeting this life truly is. It causes me to cherish each moment more deeply.

Shayla–God dropped you right into my pathway in His divine timing. The day you stepped into my life, this dream was resurrected with purpose and faith. You have been a spiritual cheerleader for me through every coffee, every breakfast and every prayer. Thank you for allowing God to use you to remind me of the impregnation of this dream.

Barb & Donald–you were the Lord's mouthpiece of prompting and promise. Thank you for being sensitive to His leading and encouraging me along the way. Donald, God gave you a dream that brought confirmation and revelation. It gave me passion to step into this. Barb, you continually hugged me and spoke life over me saying, "Don't bury your gift." I will forever be grateful for both of you.

Mary Jo–your skill, input and interest gave me a drive to just begin. Your investment into my life over the years truly led me to this moment. Watching your love for writing at a very young age, helped shape who I am today. With milky way candy bars over your thumbs, you taught me this: "Don't knock it 'till ya try it."

Mom, Marcie, Jill and Sarah–my "Spiritual Midwives," you truly have helped me give birth to this baby that felt so big. You listened to my thoughts and my rambling voice memos with patience and interest. You have nurtured this book into being. I am endlessly grateful for your support and mentorship.

Felicia–the one who dreamed with me. I'll never forget the rainy day that we were plopped down in your rows of tulips. You told me that you believed in me. And you handed me a $50 bill and said that you wanted to buy the first book. You made me believe in myself.

Charity & Christine–the ones responsible for every sketch and every poem. It has been an honor to watch you come alongside me with no reservations– using your own gifts with unique creativity. You inspired me at every turn along the way and added elements that will touch a multitude through your gifts.

My parents & siblings–the beginning of my story started with you. Pieces of my testimony today are also yours. I'm humbled by that. Thank you for always loving me, always supporting me, and always encouraging me along the way. You've been protectors of my heart through it all.

Bethany—my formatter and now friend. Thank you for your endless grace and patience to allow me to hiccup along the way—and regroup. You received me with open arms.

Lia—the one who gets all the credit for the graphic design of this book's cover. You said "yes" to me with no questions. You were patient every time I changed my mind. Thank you for taking a chance on me.

Lastly, to every reader who has made it to this page. I truly pray that you find purpose where God has planted and placed you. I pray that you find Him in every season. I pray that the touch of His Hand over your lives is recognized as the gift that it truly is.

About the Author

Melia Chapman is a woman after the heart of God. Her joy for ministry is found in leading others to know and love Jesus. This is her first self-published book. It is a compilation of her own personal life stories, along with biblical ones, that prove that God can and will meet us right where we are and restore us completely.

Melia's heart, even as a young girl, has been to sit with the lowly ones, to see the unseen ones, to carry the burdens of the burdened ones, to lift up and encourage the confused ones–the ones wrestling with a lack of identity and purpose. Most importantly, her passion is to help others discover the beauty of being rooted in the only One who is worthy of being rooted to.

God has gifted Melia with the ability for an inner radar for the lost, those without a voice. She is realizing the fullness to be found in her willingness to meet the full potential of who she was born to be–sacrificing and serving for people's lives to be saved and transformed through Jesus.

Melia lives in the Midwest with her husband Jeremy and their two sons and daughter. She loves sunsets, spending time with her family, studying and teaching God's Word, journaling, hearing people's stories, and watching the move of God's Hand over each and every day.

www.ingramcontent.com/pod-product-compliance
Lightning Source LLC
Chambersburg PA
CBHW050735010526
44107CB00010B/866